how to marry the man of your choice

REVISED AND UPDATED

MARGARET KENT

D0009024

WARNER BOOKS

NEW YORK   BOSTON

Warner Books
Time Warner Book Group
1271 Avenue of the Americas, New York, NY 10020
Visit our Web site at www.twbookmark.com.

Printed in the United States of America

First Warner Books Edition: July 1987
Revised and Updated Edition: January 2005
10 9 8 7 6 5 4 3

Library of Congress Cataloging-in-Publication Data
Kent, Margaret.
    How to marry the man of your choice / Margaret Kent. — Rev. and updated ed.
        p. cm.
    "Twentieth anniversary edition" — Pref.
    ISBN 0-446-69279-4
    1. Dating (Social customs) — United States. 2. Mate selection — United States.
3. Men — United States — Psychology. I. Title.
    HQ801.K47 2005
    646.7'7 — dc22

                                                                2004012048

Cover design by Brigid Pearson
Book design and text composition by Jo Anne Metsch

WONDERING WHY OTHER WOMEN ARE MARRIED. . .
AND YOU'RE NOT?

PUT YOUR HUSBAND HUNTING SKILLS TO THE TEST.
TRUE OR FALSE?

1. Successful marriage strategies are mental, not physical.
2. Don't waste your emotions on a man until you know he's worthy of you.
3. There are significantly more marriageable women out there than marriageable men.
4. To be successful in love, a woman must know her own strengths and be able to communicate them to her man.
5. Your ideal mate is one in a hundred, possibly one in a thousand, so you need to meet many men to find the man of your choice.
6. Despite conventional wisdom, "popular" women are not more marriageable.
7. No matter what size you wear or how fashionable you are, clothing can arouse a man's curiosity and imagination about your body.
8. Falling in love is not an endless stream of pleasant experiences.
9. "Bitchy" women get the men, and women who give true unselfish love lose out.
10. Never become involved with a man because you feel sorry for him or think you can change him.
11. Your mind is your best asset.
12. Call him. The days of a woman not calling a man are long gone.

The answers to all of these questions are true. Discover why—and learn how to stop waiting for Prince Charming to pull up to your door. Put yourself in the driver's seat, find that prince, and live happily ever after with help from HOW TO MARRY THE MAN OF YOUR CHOICE.

To my husband,

Robert Feinschreiber,

the man of my choice

Books, like marriage, don't just happen. They take planning and effort.

Much of the effort is due to my husband, Robert Feinschreiber, who encouraged me to share these marriage techniques with other women. He helped put the universality of these techniques to the test, using the United States, the former USSR, Canada, former Czechoslovakia, Japan, the United Kingdom, Australia, Hungary, Mexico, Israel, China, and Italy to challenge these techniques.

I've been fortunate to work with thoughtful editors, especially those at Warner Books. Bob Miller shepherded the first Warner edition, as Melanie Murray did with the second. I owe them both and their colleagues a great deal of gratitude.

Much of the book's success is attributable to the media itself, as they challenged and encouraged me with their extensive repartees. They did so against a backdrop of cultural and economic disparity and preconceived concepts about women and their role in securing marriage.

contents

Welcome to the twentieth-anniversary edition of *How to Marry the Man of Your Choice*. I glow with pride because the earlier editions helped millions across the world, beginning in the United States where the book spent sixteen weeks on the *New York Times* best-seller list. Here is the story behind this success.

Like most of you, I grew up expecting to have a fantastic husband, wonderful children, a spacious home, and an exciting career. These were all supposed to "just happen," as if they were "meant to be." I went to school, attended church, and made friends, but I didn't sit down to plan for my future. It wasn't until I was in my twenties that I decided to take full charge of my life—including marriage.

My father, Jack Bradfield, left New Jersey and came to Miami in 1926, back when nobody bothered to count the horses in town. My mother, Hilda Arechavaleta, arrived a decade later from Havana; they married in October 1941.

I was born in Miami in the late summer of 1942, at the height of World War II. My father was concerned about our safety during the war, and often sent my mother and me back to Cuba.

We had a large family in Havana, where my great-uncle was an ambassador from Cuba to various countries. His children pursued careers in law and medicine, but I planned to follow in his footsteps.

My life was moving ahead idyllically as 1958 came to an end. I prepared myself for high school graduation and attendance at a faraway distant university to study diplomacy. Thoughts of marriage were long off in the future.

Then in 1959, it happened. Castro seized power in Cuba and announced that he was a communist. Neither property nor people were safe. The time for hopes and dreams was over. I had to go to Cuba to help rescue my family. We evaded the gunfire from Castro's army and eventually made our way to safety.

Our house in Miami was a small one, adequate for my parents and myself. Now we were deluged with uncles, aunts, cousins, and our older relatives. I never knew what sleeping in shifts meant until then. My plans for European travel and foreign study were long dashed. Many of my relatives spoke no English and were still suffering from the shock and horrors of the Castro takeover. I was needed on the home front, so I enrolled at the inexpensive Barry University and went to work nearly full time for the telephone company.

I was twenty when I finished college and began teaching at a high school and adult education programs in Miami. I undertook my graduate studies in Mexico at Tecnológico de Monterrey, and my social life began. I started thinking about marriage. I knew that good things wouldn't happen without effort and planning, but I didn't yet have the specific skills I needed to plan for marriage. I pondered why many undeserving women (in my opinion) had great guys, and so many deserving women (in my opinion) did not. I wondered:

➤ Why do women attract men they don't want?
➤ Why don't women attract men they do want?
➤ Why is it so difficult to meet men?
➤ Why do men appear to reject marriage?
➤ What do men really want?

I realized there were many wonderful women who wanted marriage, but it wasn't happening for them. Worse yet, many of these women were in their thirties and forties. Statistics demonstrated the grim possibility of marriage at their ages, with odds for marriage diminishing each successive year. As these and many other questions about marriage came to mind, I decided to seek the answers.

In 1967, I was teaching Spanish and French in high school, and English and Spanish in adult education programs. One of my evening students in the Spanish-language program was George Kent. He was originally a Jesuit and engineer, and later became a lawyer and psychiatrist. George had a number of Spanish-speaking patients and clients, and asked me to be his translator.

As an attorney, George had a number of female clients who had been left by their husbands after long marriages and were distressed about their prospects. As a psychiatrist, he had a number of patients who were single women and despondent over their marriage chances. As I worked with George, I realized that there was a pattern to these marriage problems. I decided to turn these patterns into a strategy and use them to marry George, with whom I had fallen in love.

I put my plan into effect in September 1968. By Christmas, George had made a commitment to me. We were engaged on Valentine's Day in 1969 and married that June.

Many of my friends heard about my success with George and asked me to help them. I put together a marriage course for six of them, and they each married about six months after the course ended.

Some four hundred people have completed the course between 1969 and 1979. Every single one of the four hundred was married within four years, and most were married within two. I began to formulate a comprehensive marriage strategy, which was to have two foundations:

1. The marriage strategy must comprehensively address all facets of the marriage process. The marriage strategy, then,

begins before the woman meets men for dating, and carries forward through the dating process, the selection process, the wedding process, and beyond, to sustain a happy marriage. I was all too aware that many marriage advice books addressed only one facet of the marriage process, such as meeting men, or wedding planning, but failed to provide the women with the techniques to move from meeting men to the wedding. I sought to fill out that monumental gap.

2. The marriage strategy must be universal, applying to civilized cultures and giving due deference to economic circumstances, religion, and culture. I later had the opportunity to put my marriage techniques into practice with *How to Marry the Man of Your Choice* in the United States, Canada, Great Britain, Mexico, Brazil, Italy, Ireland, and then in the USSR (before the end of the communist period), and postcommunist Russia. The Czech Republic, Hungary, China, Israel, and Japan came afterward. The need for this material on a global basis was astonishing! *How to Marry the Man of Your Choice* has been distributed in more than thirty countries. Women, no matter what their culture is, often have difficulty marrying the man of their choice.

My first marriage ended tragically. George's unexpected death in 1979 sent me into deep mourning for more than a year. Then I decided it was time to start living again and find another great husband—despite the fact that I was almost forty! I began law school in 1980, completed it in 1983, and became an attorney in Florida.

I met Robert Feinschreiber, a renowned tax expert, on December 30, 1981. We married December 30, 1984. Although the marriage process I advocate usually takes two years, it took me three. Why? Well, I didn't start going out with Robert until more than a year and a half after meeting him.

Of course, I used the marriage strategy again with Robert. He is so smart, he sensed it. Often he would say, "I know you are doing something different; promise me you won't ever stop."

Thanks to Robert, you have this book in your hands: He shepherded the material from my technical, psychologically based course materials into a privately published book and then to Warner Books. Robert developed a masterful marketing plan: a husband or your money back. Warner returned just 0.02 percent.

Many major talk shows invited me as a guest, often more than once. I was Oprah Winfrey's first guest when her Chicago talk show went national! Phil Donahue, Larry King, Geraldo Rivera, Regis Philbin, Montel Williams, Joan Rivers, Sally Jessy Raphael, and Maury Povich are among my other most favorite U. S. interviewers, together with Tom Charrington in Canada, Terry Wogan in the United Kingdom, and Gay Byrne in Ireland. Then there were Spanish-language shows, including *Cristina*, *Sabado Gigante*, and *Despierta America*.

Like many of you, I have multifaceted interests, and do other things in life. I practice law in Florida with Robert, focusing on divorce, wills and probate, and discrimination cases, tax work, and export incentives. We have also been participating in the privatization of economies in countries formerly part of the USSR. The UN sends us on missions. I've had the unusual privilege of dining at the Kremlin on various occasions and visiting Russia's former secret atomic city.

It's my pleasure to help women all over the world. I hope that this book makes your search for a mate easy and as enjoyable as it should be! The strategies are effective, and a great deal of fun for both the man and the woman. Men will enjoy their dates with you more than ever, and you'll enjoy your quest. You'll especially love how your confidence with men increases. Write me about your experiences with this material at multijur@aol.com or through my Web site, www.RomanceRoad.com. Send me an announcement of your wedding!

Look around you, and observe other women. You'll see women who aren't as attractive, youthful, slim, bright, educated, or successful as you. But some of these women have men you might want. You may think these women are absolutely undesirable, yet they are married. Why are they married while you're still single?

How to Marry the Man of Your Choice reveals the secrets behind the success these other women have with men. It will show you the techniques you can use in meeting men, developing relationships, and leading the man of your choice into marriage.

You don't *have* to stay single. These strategies will lead you out of the singles jungle and into a happy marriage with the man of your choice. The twelve chapters show you the steps to follow to success.

Finding a mate should be a thrilling adventure. The purpose of *How to Marry the Man of Your Choice* is to make that adventure easy and successful. The book is designed for all women seeking marriage, including women for whom the marriage process is mysterious or befuddling.

THE PROCESS OF FALLING IN LOVE

How to Marry the Man of Your Choice shows you how the marriage process works and how you can use it to your advantage. I'll analyze and apply the specific steps in the love process. I'll show you how to initiate and nurture the relationship with the man you're seeking for your husband.

The operative phrase in the title of the book is *your choice*. If the man you're with is not the man of your choice, move on. Even if your goal is just to increase your dating skills, this book will help.

Love is much more than infatuation. Falling in love is not an endless stream of pleasant experiences. It may surprise you, but the process of falling in love is similar in many ways to the process through which individuals become believers in a religious faith or become patriots to a country. I will examine all aspects of the love process. I'll show you techniques that will help your fellow fall zealously in love with you.

You will learn strategies based on the principles of psychology, law, psychiatry, religion, and many other professions. These techniques show you how human behavior can be predicted, molded, influenced, and controlled. The book integrates the theories of these behavioral sciences to provide you with advice aimed specifically at leading a desirable man into marriage. If you use these concepts, you should achieve great success with men, and be able to marry the man of your choice.

Use these techniques to facilitate the natural process by which people fall in love. This book is designed for the woman who wants to have a man fall in love with her and marry her, but whose own skills in obtaining the man she wants are inadequate.

If you're worried that the strategies are clinical and there will be no fun in your quest, be assured that just the opposite is true. You will experience emotional highs from the successes you will achieve.

HOW TO SUCCEED WITH MEN

Doesn't it seem to you that the bitchy women get the men, and that the women who give true unselfish love lose out? If this is the way you view the world of love, you are viewing it accurately, and I will explain why your perception is correct. Bitchy women succeed with men because they make them believe that they are superior women, and that a man is lucky to have them. You will learn how to make a man feel honored that you love him.

EVALUATING MEN

One of the primary causes for marriage failure is that people do not adequately know the individuals they marry. We *meet* strangers, which is fine, but we often *marry* strangers based on assumptions about them we've never tested. The result is an invitation to disaster. My techniques are designed to help you get to know the man as he really is. Better a curtailed dating relationship than a broken marriage. The best surprise in marriage is no surprise.

Dating is your opportunity to evaluate your dates and create the bonding that leads to marriage. Don't spend your date time just having fun. Enjoy being with your fellow, but do this after you evaluate him and the prospects for your future together.

When a man contemplates marriage to a specific woman, he evaluates her as a prospective wife. Don't be ashamed of evaluating the men you meet as prospective husbands.

You may worry that your evaluation process will be too conscious and rational, but all too often it's unconscious and irrational, as well as haphazard and incomplete. Sharpen your ability to evaluate men and use your evaluations in selecting the man you want to marry.

It isn't safe to invest your emotions in a stranger. You would certainly do some checking before you invested large sums with someone you didn't know. Aren't your emotions worth at least as much? If so, investigate before you invest.

Don't waste your emotions on a man until you determine that he's worthy of you. Never become involved with a man because you feel sorry for him or think you can change him.

Don't be a closet heterosexual. If you want to meet and marry the man of your choice, you've got to go public. Let the world know you like men! Be active, not passive, in your quest.

Marrying a Stranger

Marrying is much more complicated than it used to be. We face different issues than our ancestors did. They did not marry strangers. They most typically came from a small village or farming community and rarely traveled far from home. Community members were inculcated in the same values, and shared the same language, religion, background, and culture. Often families lived in the same area for generation after generation. Even if a bride and groom did not know each other, the families knew each other and could predict a couple's compatibility.

Few among us would marry a total stranger. Yet some of us marry virtual strangers, those who might lack the commonalities that make a marriage work. We might not know a man's ingrained values or scruples, including religion, family values, patriotism, goals, zeniths, interpersonal relations, work ethic, and emotional events, unless we probe and verify.

Our ancestors had a narrower field of choice in marriage, with fewer chances to commit errors. With the opportunities we have today, there is a greater probability we'll make wrong decisions. Thus it's incumbent on us to learn more about our potential spouses than our ancestors did.

Transportation and communications advances have put us increasingly into contact with strangers. The telephone, automobiles, and the Internet have all increased the likelihood that we'll meet new people. Your horizons are broader than ever, making it important that you know your prospective spouse better than ever to make a thoughtful and wise choice.

The Myth of the Infinite Universe

Some women act as if there is an infinite universe of eligible men. These women have detailed, specific demands for their ideal mates, as if they were building a home from scratch and had an unlimited supply of funds and patience.

The myth of the infinite universe causes many of us to act carelessly and thoughtlessly. We gave short shrift to the men we meet, believing that more and better men lie ahead. We gave many prospective mates no more thought than we would give to a grain of sand on the beach, treating the supply of prospective mates as infinite.

Beyond Fairy Tales and Fantasies

If you're old enough to be contemplating marriage, you should be mature enough to put fairy tales and fantasies behind you. Do you really think that all good things will come to you if you wish hard enough or wait long enough? Fairy tales do all of us a disservice because they teach a woman to be passive. Yet all too often, the silly tales of our childhood linger in our minds, especially when it comes to marriage.

Some women believe that men are all frogs waiting to be turned into princes. They think of themselves as Sleeping Beauty, waiting to be found and awakened. They should realize that the man with the glass slipper is just a shoe salesman, and that glass is a dangerous material for slippers.

START WITH YOURSELF

Take charge of your own life, of being all that you want to be, including being happily married to the man of your choice.

Your mind is your best asset, for it can improve with use. Everything else eventually sags, wrinkles, or turns gray. The crucial marriage strategies are mental, not physical. Don't make marriage decisions with just one part of your body, whether it's between your legs or behind your ribs. Use your head.

As a starting point, recognize that you are a worthwhile individual. You don't need anyone, whether man or institution, to validate your self-worth. Don't let anyone tell you otherwise.

Your self-worth, however, is not self-evident. Don't expect the world at large, especially the men in it, to recognize how wonderful you are, at least without a little prompting on your part. It's time for you to take the initiative.

You don't need marriage to give you a sense of self-worth. Then, you may ask, why marry? Because marriage can be fun and enrich your life. You may be a woman who has everything you want—except a husband.

Why So Much Work? Shouldn't You Just "Be Yourself"?

As you read this book, you will be asking yourself, *Why do I have to expend so much effort? What about the man? Why isn't he pursuing me?* Let's answer these questions now.

There are significantly more marriageable women than marriageable men. If marriage is a priority in your life and you have passed the age at which the marriage odds are in your favor, you need updated techniques. The odds were greatly in your favor during your teenage years and early twenties, but they increasingly turn against you as you get older. You can't sit around like a beached whale, waiting for the tides to come in with your bounty. All you'll get is dead fish and seaweed.

But shouldn't I just be myself, and act naturally? Yes, be yourself, but be yourself at your best. You may be wonderful, but even *you* can benefit from greater confidence. You don't need to change your personality. Instead, improve your skills in dealing with men.

The Gripers

Over the years, *How to Marry the Man of Your Choice* was well received around the world. I met women across the globe, and the book sold more than a million copies, yet a few women objected to certain precepts in the book. I take seriously any negative comments I heard more than once, and have responded to them.

Complaint 1: "Your marriage techniques require me to put in too much effort. I would never put that much effort into marrying—or doing anything else in my life, for that matter. Can't you somehow simplify this marriage process?"

My response: Marrying takes a great deal of effort, both in leading your fellow to marriage and in securing a long-term successful relationship. There are no easy solutions to making a marriage work. Don't seek marriage if you feel it's not worth the effort you'll have to put in.

Complaint 2: "Your marrying techniques tell me to change myself. I'm quite fine as I am—close to perfect, in fact. What I need is for men to change, so that they can better meet my needs."

My response: I'll help you learn the strategies you'll need to help your man change his behavior in your favor. You don't need to change your values or your inner core in your marriage quest.

Complaint 3: "I date to have fun. I enjoy movies and theater. Listening to men talk about themselves isn't what I call a date. I want to do what I want to do. Your book takes the fun out of dating."

My response: If you don't enjoy finding out about your man, or if you consider movies or the theater more important than knowing men, you're not ready for marriage. You are only playing at a relationship. You, like some men, are dating for reasons other than marriage.

Complaint 4: "You tell me to listen to what men are saying, and then encourage them to talk. But this fellow bores me to tears."

My response: If he bores you now, think of how much more boring he'll be later. Move on, quickly. He's not the man of your choice.

Complaint 5: "Where's the magic pill, the magic potion? I want to get married *now!*"

My response: Don't rush. If your choice is wrong, you may be stuck. There's no magic pill here. Success in anything requires effort, whether that's weight loss, schooling, or career. This is true in marriage, too.

Complaint 6: "I want the man to cater to me the way young men used to do. Guys used to chase after me, bring me flowers and more. What's wrong with guys nowadays anyway?"

My response: Your parents may have raised you to believe that you're a goddess, but you'll have to come down to earth before you can soar with your fellow. I'm sorry to tell you this, but the male–female relationship changed after puberty. Pampering ends with adulthood.

Complaint 7: "Why do I need your help in getting married? I can get married at any time, at any place, and with whomever I choose!"

My response: I'm helping you become better at what you do, to enhance your skills and use them in the art and skill of marrying the man of your choice. If you really were successful in all that you do, and you wanted marriage, you'd long ago have been married.

Complaint 8: "Look at me! I'm absolutely gorgeous! I demand expensive restaurants, gifts, and much more. Your book does not help me get the lavish dates that I'm seeking."

My response: Seeking to become a trophy wife is risky, because you can easily be replaced by next year's model. I'm helping real women seeking real marriage instead.

A very few men objected to the underlying premise of this book, which is that women have a choice: Women have the right to marry or not, and they have the choice of whom they marry. These objectors would deny women such choices and treat them as chattel. Better eliminate these men quickly from your dating pool!

What Do You Offer a Man?

Ask a woman what she wants in a man, and she is likely to have specific answers. She may want a tall, handsome, youthful, intelligent, rich, witty, respectful, capable, educated man of a particular background. Ask the same woman what she can offer him in exchange, and her answer is usually, "Me."

"Me" is a poor, unspecific answer. The woman must evaluate herself against her competitors. To be successful with her man, she must know what she has to offer and be able to communicate it to the man.

If you are still thinking, *I just want to be me!* consider what happens when you go into a restaurant and order a cup of coffee. You don't expect it to be free because "This cup of coffee is for *me!*" If you know that "me" is not going to get you a free cup of coffee, why would it get you a mate? Being yourself, and doing nothing more, isn't going to get you anything in life, especially the mate you desire.

A Few Words About Manipulation

This book examines the techniques of manipulation. You will learn how to manipulate others, and how to prevent others from manipulating you without your knowledge. But, you ask, *Isn't manipulation bad?*

Manipulation is all around us. We are manipulated by our parents, loved ones, teachers, churches, advertisers, bosses, government, and others. Sometimes we're manipulated for our own good, as is the case, for instance, with wearing seat belts. Even here, there are many facets to the manipulation: The name *seat belts* was changed to *safety belts*, laws impose fines for not buckling up, and public-service announcements educate us. The techniques described in this book are benign manipulation, much like the incentives to use seat belts or the star your teacher put on your paper to encourage you to keep up the good work.

At numerous points throughout this book, I urge you to remain silent and encourage the man to talk. This is not meekness or coyness, but an important manipulative principle. The person who listens first and speaks second has the advantage because she knows what the first person has said and can respond accordingly. Let others call this manipulation if they like. If the word bothers you, just call it common sense.

Hot and Calculating

The strategies you will learn are rational and analytical. I'm not teaching you how to lust after someone, to swoon, or to make your heart palpitate with excitement. These emotions are an important facet of a relationship, but I hope and assume that you already have them, or can recognize them when you feel them.

I don't want you to diminish your emotions, or put them aside. Reason and logic alone are not sufficient motivation for marrying someone, but emotion alone shouldn't be sufficient, either.

Use both your head and your heart in accepting or rejecting someone for marriage. Reason and emotion should both say yes before you proceed to the altar.

These marriage strategies are not cold and calculating; they are hot and calculating. Passion and logic are *both* essential.

How Important Is Popularity?

Are you striving to be popular with men? Do you believe that popularity will make you more marriageable? If so, pause and reevaluate your strategy.

Don't try to please everyone, for you may end up then pleasing no one. Don't try to be all things to all people. You are seeking that one special person, not running for office.

Women, remember that you are more selective than the marines. They're looking for a few good men, but you're looking for just one.

Take the Initiative

How to Marry the Man of Your Choice is designed only for women who want to take charge of their future when it comes to marriage. Take this simple quiz:

1. If you wanted to succeed in drama, you would:
   a. *Wait to be discovered.*
   b. *Take drama lessons.*
2. If you had money to invest, you would:
   a. *Buy lottery tickets.*
   b. *Invest in stocks, bonds, or real estate.*

3. If you wanted to become wealthy, you would:
   a. *Wish for a windfall.*
   b. *Put your ideas to work.*
4. If you wanted to be president, you would:
   a. *Hope to be sought out.*
   b. *Enter politics.*
5. If you wanted marriage, you would:
   a. *Expect to find a husband on your doorstep.*
   b. *Look for a man to marry.*

Examine your answers to these five questions. If you've marked b's rather than a's, you would have taken drama lessons if you wanted to succeed in drama, invested if you could in stocks, bonds, or real estate, put your ideas to work if you wanted to become wealthy, entered politics if you wanted to be president, and looked for a man who would be your husband if you wanted marriage.

If your answers are predominantly a's, not b's, however, do us both a favor and don't buy this book. You may very well wind up sitting at home alone on Saturday night, waiting for magic to happen while others who have less to offer are pursuing and catching someone who could be suitable for you.

Forget the old myth that you can't find love when you're looking for it. The key is to know where and how to look. Many women have come to believe this myth after getting all dressed up for a social event and meeting no one, and then meeting a man when they're wearing nothing more than jeans and a T-shirt. Yes, this happens, but it does *not* mean you shouldn't look for love. It simply means you must learn to look differently. You *can* look for love—and find it. Love is too important to be left to happenstance.

Why not make your life as pleasurable as possible? Your goal should be to move toward pleasure and away from pain. The amount of pleasure you receive will be your mark of success. If you would enjoy having a husband, don't let anyone deter you from this pleasure.

USING THE MATERIAL

You are going to attract many men using the *How to Marry the Man of Your Choice* marriage strategy. Continue the strategy only on the man you want. This book is not meant to turn you into a heartbreaker; it's intended to minimize the risk of someone breaking your heart.

These techniques are powerful. Be sure you want the man before you lead him into marriage. If you apply all the techniques to a man you don't want, you may find that you've painted yourself into a corner!

These strategies are designed for women of all ages (eighteen and older) who can use them consistently. You don't need to be physically perfect to use these methods, but you do need to be psychologically healthy. Of course, make sure the man you select is psychologically healthy, too.

Evaluate the methods and strategies, if any, that you now use with men. As you learn this book's techniques and achieve your marriage potential, you'll find yourself changing your behavior with men. Make note of these changes, for they are important to your further development.

For maximum benefits to you, read *How to Marry the Man of Your Choice* with an open mind. Let it imprint its ideas on you without objections, at least until you have completed your training. If you need proof that the material is valid and effective, don't fight the ideas—test them! But be sure to apply your test correctly. There's usually a large gap between what men do and what they say they do, so be wary of believing in surveys of male attitudes. Go by behavior instead.

You need to recognize when you are succeeding, especially when the man's behavior is fluctuating. You need to know the reasons for praising and criticizing a man. You need courage and guidance to discuss your self-esteem and importance to him.

If you review this material often, and you practice what you read, you should become increasingly successful with men. Whenever you achieve some success with a concept, review the material. You may discover a subconcept that you have overlooked or ignored. Continue to apply these concepts as you reach new heights in your relationships with men. You can develop a zest for winning in your manhunt.

Use Your Time Wisely

Choosing a man for marriage requires considerable effort. To marry well, you need to make good use of your time and your abilities. Since you cannot sift men through giant colanders, you must sift them through your life by learning about them. Then you can pick and choose the best. It's all about choice. That's the essence of freedom.

It is impractical, impossible, and injurious to your health and wealth to entertain all the men you meet with the traditional routines of food and drink, sex and sweets. Besides, this is the most unlikely way to find and marry the man of your choice.

Don't ignore the selection process and rush into marriage. An unrestrained pursuit of wedlock may lead to a faster marriage, but after the excitement is over, you may realize that with a little patience you could have chosen more wisely. If you are serious about marriage and you apply the techniques of this book in a consistent manner, it should take you less than two years to meet and marry the man of your choice.

Your Marriage Strategy

Apply the chapters in order. Chapter 1 teaches you about men, and chapter 2 shows you how to attract them. Chapter 3 tells you how and where you can meet men, and chapter 4 helps you get more out of dating. Chapter 5 tells you how to interview a man for the job of husband before you audition for the job of wife. Then, if you encourage a man to keep on talking and tell you the events in his life that have emotional meaning, he will talk his way into love with you. Chapter 6 explores the specifics.

You didn't tell all those strange men you met the intimacies of your life, but what do you say to the man you *do* want? Chapter 7 gives you the advice you need to help you enhance your self-esteem and present yourself in a more positive manner.

Praise and criticism are a part of daily life, and essential for the person you are considering as a prospective spouse. Chapter 8 explores these crucial techniques. Chapter 9 tells you how to cope with arguments and foibles you'll face while bonding.

Since marriage is a sexual relationship, you need to know how to use sex to your advantage in leading your relationship to marriage. Chapter 10 tells you how. Chapter 11 helps you avoid common mistakes that frighten off men just before the wedding. Chapter 12 shows you specific strategies for the engagement and wedding itself.

Developing Your Action Plan

As you read this book, think of the ways you can apply these strategies in your own personal situation. There is no one quite like you, no one with exactly the same desires, needs, interests, or taste in men. Consequently, you need to know yourself, what you seek in a mate, and what you have to offer. Then develop your own action plan to personalize your marriage strategy.

How to Marry the Man of Your Choice provides advice for women seeking marriage. The book provides marriage procedures that depend on the reader's ability and effort to apply those techniques to the circumstances we observed. Success depends on your own efforts! Happy husband hunting!

chapter 1

Learning About Men

The more you know about men in general, the easier it will be to learn about individual men. The more you know how men think and behave, the more success you'll have with the men you meet. There are three keys to male behavior:

1. The typical man has been predominantly influenced by women during his formative years. As a result, he has predictable reactions to women.
2. A man bases his sense of sexual worth and acceptance as a male on his teenage experiences. He carries that sexual acceptance or rejection to the grave.
3. The male ego is enormous, but eggshell-fragile. Learn about the male ego. Your knowledge of his ego is one of the best tools for leading the man of your choice into a long-term relationship.

WHAT YOU NEED TO KNOW

Is men's behavior a mystery to you? Here's the three-step process to unlocking this mystery and using it to your advantage:

1. Learn about usual male behavior.
2. Use this knowledge to predict the behavior of the men you meet.

3. Use a man's own behavior as a means of leading him into a long-term relationship with you.

WHY MEN ACT THE WAY THEY DO

Males are under the authority and guidance of females from the beginning. They are born of woman and are helpless from birth until years later. From his earliest moments, the young boy is forced into behavior that pleases his mother, female relatives, and female teachers. Each one has a turn at subjecting the boy to her ideas of acceptable behavior, demeanor, and thoughts. As a youngster, he is dependent on his mother and other female relatives for his comfort and survival. He remains dependent on women for much of his comfort and survival throughout his life.

Schooling generally is painful for the boy. His female teachers embarrass him with their authority, his subjugation to them, and his mental limitations. His female classmates impress him with their maturity and perhaps faster understanding of the classwork. If the boy rebels, a principal dictates that his teachers, who are likely to be mostly female, place the boy under their greater control.

Because of the boy's slower physical development, female classmates usually scorn him until they reach puberty. The girls can do so freely, since at that age they don't need these boys sexually. This type of intense and prolonged conditioning is hard for these boys to overcome, even when they mature.

Puberty

The male–female relationship begins to change at puberty. Girls at adolescence begin to experience sexual curiosity and desire. They start competing with each other for the attention and affection of the more desirable boys.

Adolescent males, on the other hand, are supposed to surmount their years of conditioning to subservient childhood status by nature alone. The boy is expected to become the sexual initiator. Older or faster-maturing boys in his class cause the lad to declare his emancipation from female control. These boys call the less mature youth a sissy or a mommy's boy if women continue to dominate his life. Yet these same women despise this fellow if they continue to dominate him once he becomes an adult.

His Teenage Years

The teenage years are called the formative years. Most boys feel particularly awkward and unattractive in the early teenage years. His height increases rapidly in an ungainly manner. His face is filled with pimples, and braces cover his teeth. His self-image is likely to be low because girls reject his advances. The male develops his self-image at precisely this period. His acceptability and his acceptance among females are at their lowest. Yet it's at this time in his life that he needs female companionship the most, as sexuality begins and reaches its peak. This sharp disparity between the male's needs and his actual relationships gives the male a negative self-image.

As a survival technique, the man asserts that he is tough, invincible, and unique. The man develops his ego in part because of his rapid increase in strength and height. His ego is largely a facade. His ego is eggshell-fragile because it is self-generated.

Dating

Dating is cruel to both men and women. Consider the following:

Men with high sex drives most often have unfulfilled sexual needs. Consequently, these men have especially negative self-images. Such a man suffers most when women reject him. His sensitivity to rejection causes him a horrible predicament. He can't hide his drive; nor can he afford to spend his time dating a woman without achieving sexual satisfaction. Yet women often view his sexual aggression as an affront to their dignity. He wants her, but she'll scorn him as a boor or worse.

A woman is often more receptive to men who are well mannered and polite, men who go through life with a minimum level of hormonal disruption and conform to society's mores. But these men are often those who lack sexual interest in women. These men tend to have low sex drives and a lower level of unfulfilled needs. These men suffer less during their teenage years. As adults, these men often appear gentlemanly and patient in initiating a sexual encounter. A woman may want such a man, but then puzzle over his lack of sexual interest in her.

Reversing of Dating Fortune

Females do well in their early years for three reasons:

1. The higher male birthrate, which increases the demand for females for pairing
2. The higher male sex drive at that age bracket.
3. The acceptability in our society for young women to date men somewhat older than themselves.

These factors give the man a low self-image and give the woman a high self-image. But these self-images become increasingly inappropriate as the individuals mature. In fact, these self-images will hinder relationships in the future unless women and men correct them. The situation reverses as time goes on because of three factors:

1. Women outlive men.
2. Women's sex drives increase later than men's.
3. Women face increasing competition from younger women.

Women are well advised to understand these facts. Their teenage years are behind them, and so is the attention that young men paid to them.

Rites of Passage to Adulthood

When does adulthood occur? Often it's at the moment of getting the car keys, because of the freedom that a car provides. The car is the youth's first kingdom. With his car, a youth controls where he wants to be and with whom, and his degree of privacy. His car may be as important to him as the family home is to his parents. The car is a status symbol that represents power, money, prestige, and independence, and buttresses the youth's self-esteem. The fellow who lacked a car in his formative years is going to be quite a different person from the guy who had wheels as a young man. Chances are that the carless youth is burdened with even lower self-esteem.

As a rule of thumb, whatever the man lacked or thought he lacked in his formative years, he will seek during the rest of his life. If the boy could not afford to dress as well as his friends, as an adult he will strive for an expensive wardrobe. Conversely, if the boy had more than adequate clothes, as a man he won't be particularly concerned about clothing.

Familiarities and Fantasies

Women often have a very difficult time unshackling themselves from the attitude of scorn they felt toward the men whom they first knew as youngsters. It's rare that a woman marries a man she knew at that age. Even if a woman marries someone she grew up with, they were probably apart during their formative years.

On an Israeli kibbutz, the parents are particularly eager for their youngsters to grow up together and be familiar with each other from youth. These parents put their youngsters together so that they can marry more wisely. Surprisingly, the parents find that these close childhood friends rarely wed. These youngsters know each other's weaknesses. They aren't impressed with each other's facades. We must marry strangers, for only strangers appear to measure up to our illusions.

WHAT IS A MAN?

Men generally behave in a consistent manner and share similar attitudes. Below, you'll find a list of some of these characteristics; the more typical the man, the more these general guides will apply to him. Not every characteristic applies to every man, but most will apply to most men. After all, the conventional male has been conditioned to certain conduct and behavior. As an adult man, he has consistent thought patterns and a stable self-image that make his behavior predictable. His self-image results from what others have said to him over the years, how they have acted toward him, and the limited freedom he has managed to achieve.

Depending on how closely your man fits the male pattern, here's what you can expect:

> ➤ He is a small boy at heart.
> ➤ He has a public facade that differs from his natural behavior.
> ➤ He inherently prefers a good marriage to being single.
> ➤ He is conditioned to obey women, starting with his mother.
> ➤ He will enjoy being led into marriage, except by foul and dastardly acts.
> ➤ He is polygamous by nature, but he learns to be monogamous by conditioning.
> ➤ He is very possessive about his mate and will extend himself considerably to keep her.
> ➤ He will attempt to follow the mores and the laws of the society in which he lives.
> ➤ He will follow social customs of his community.
> ➤ He is likely to believe in a higher power.
> ➤ He believes that he is inferior in many ways to other men.

➤ He will work to earn a living.

➤ His views follow popular notions.

➤ He likes sports—participating, watching, or both.

➤ He is not likely to believe in astrology or in fortune-telling.

➤ He wants and desires to be thought of as a lover.

➤ When ill, he will seek care from a woman who loves him.

➤ He usually will hold himself out as being better than his co-workers or peers, even when he is equal or lower in stature or achievement.

➤ He is slightly braver than his mate, and will defend her against physical attacks by others.

➤ Sooner or later, he wants children.

➤ He believes that he is special or unique.

➤ He will marry a woman only if she recognizes that he is special or unique.

➤ He expects more praise than criticism, but does expect both.

➤ He enjoys talking about himself.

➤ He expects convenient sex in marriage; in fact, it may be a principal reason he marries.

You can better anticipate a man's actions by learning these general features of male behavior. If a man says something that contradicts these attributes—say, that he will never marry—it may be wise to disregard his words. If most of the above statements apply to a man, he is likely to be available for marriage—unless he's married already.

A particular man will rarely have every single one of these typical attitudes. Trust that your fellow has normal behavior unless you have clear and convincing evidence to the contrary. Your man is likely to be as similar to other men, and as distinct from them, as you are similar to and yet distinct from other women as a group.

Your Man as an Individual

You might not know what behavior you can expect from a man in a specific situation. If his actions offend you because they are so different from the typical man's, he usually won't hold your response against you for long. He should understand that your reaction is a normal one. If you express ideas that he doesn't share, a common reaction on his part is to attempt to convince you of the merits of his beliefs so that you'll accept or understand him.

Determine how your man deviates from "typical" conduct by carefully observing his behavior and his choice of friends and attitudes. For example, if your man is a nudist, he obviously has scorned society's taboos on nudity. What you then must deal with is whether you could live with or become a nudist. If your man is an atheist, could you bring up children without religious values? How much does he care what others think of him socially? Could you love him if he insists on always expressing his thoughts even if it could start a public rift or family fight? Would you want this man to be your husband?

IDEAL MATES

Our society has rules that run contrary to nature. The typical female's ideal of what she wants in a man is vastly different from the actual men she meets. Her dream man is likely to be a combination of father image, movie idol, and a character out of novels.

In many instances, not just in husband hunting, people do not know what they really want. One woman had owned many homes because her husband was a contractor. She decided to have her husband build her an ideal house comprising all the features she liked best in each of the houses she had owned. The outcome was a horror, even to her, because the ideas clashed.

Chances are that if you meet your ideal mate or a better man than you could imagine, you would not truly want him for marriage! Sit down and make yourself a checklist of the characteristics you want in a man. Then list the positive and negative effects each characteristic would have on you. Think carefully about what you want or need so that your list is realistic.

You might be seeking Tony's ability to entertain, David's high sex drive, and Chuck's dedication to one woman all rolled up into your next guy. In fact, while Tony does enjoy entertaining, this might mean he'd rather be hosting a party than having a quiet cup of coffee with you discussing your private lives. Likewise, David's high sex drive can mean that he is attracted to many women, not dedicated to only one. Chuck's dedication to one woman may mean that his sex drive is on the low side, and one woman is all he can handle.

Evaluate the characteristics you insist upon in a man, then double-check the downside of each and how much will it bother you. Confirm that this is what you want in a man before you shop for one.

chapter 2

Dressing for Sexess

When you go out to meet men, do you go as is? Or do you take a shower, fix your hair, put on makeup, and dress in a way you think will enhance your appeal? If so, you're using your looks to manipulate men. This chapter will help you use the power of clothing more effectively.

Don't let the power of clothing pass you by. Clothing can be your major asset in competing with other women. If you are afraid to read further because you have limited funds or a body that's not quite fit for fashion, don't worry. As you'll see, you don't need thin thighs to marry the man of your choice. Dressing to attract men has nothing to do with fashion or size. It means using clothing to arouse a man's curiosity and his imagination about your body.

Sexuality is primarily a state of mind. If you've ever visited a nudist camp, you know that the clothed body is more sensuous than the nude body. There's even a joke about a male nudist who, before leaving the office early one afternoon, calls up his wife and says, "Honey, I'm horny and coming home, so get dressed!" Wearing no clothing at all leaves nothing to the imagination.

Don't feel guilty about using your appearance to attract men. You're not going to create a relationship under false pretenses. You'll be noticed by men, and will not scare them off. You'll increase your new relationships and a chance to prosper at love.

FOR WHOM DO YOU DRESS?

Answer this question honestly. For whom do you really dress? If your answer is "other women," then you aren't dressing in a way that appeals to men. If you dress to impress other women, your clothes are working against you, not for you, in your quest for an ideal mate. Other women may indeed be impressed by the sophistication of the design, the creativity of the designer, or the money you spent in purchasing your outfit. These design factors don't impress most men, though.

Fashion can enhance your appearance, but it's hard for most women to know which fashions have a positive effect on men. Chances are, you were taken shopping by your mother and waited on by a saleswoman. If you never had male input, you probably don't know what clothing appeals to men.

If you dress for clients or business, then your business clothes probably emulate men's clothing. The major difference between your suits and a man's suits is that his have pants and yours probably have skirts. If this is your situation, you need a separate social wardrobe.

Dress Friendly

Many women dress properly for men when they're not paying attention to their clothing. When these women aren't focusing on their clothes, they wear cotton solid-color T-shirts and simple straight skirts or jeans. Men find these women sexy. All too often, women look like mannequins wrapped in lace or unnatural nightwear when they dress for a date.

Select your wardrobe carefully, as it can be a real plus in attracting men. Your goal is to dress to attract a man for a long-term relationship. Stir his sexual imagination about you. You're not satisfying his curiosity about your body with a see-through blouse or a wet T-shirt. You're stirring his imagination by showing easy access to sexy body areas instead. The catchphrase is *dress friendly*. You can give him permission to touch you later.

Let Him Choose

If your man wants to select your clothes, let him! Give him the choice for a fun date. You could let him select clothing that would make you more appealing. You could do the same with his wardrobe.

DRESSING TO ATTRACT MEN

If you want to dress to attract men for a long-term relationship, here's some good advice on twenty different style issues.

1. Cleanliness

Cleanliness is especially important. If you have the clean, fresh look that comes from a recent shower, you can wear a potato sack and still be desirable.

2. Follow Your Body Lines

What do you think when you see a man in a plaid suit, red-striped shirt, polka-dot tie, and white socks? No doubt you view him as a nerd and reject him. Yet this man may be expending a great deal of effort to meet women. In fact, he may be dressing the way he does to gain your attention! It may surprise you, but women can make the same types of errors in their wardrobe. Women can be nerds, too.

Here are some tips that can keep a man from viewing you as a nerd. Wear clothing that follows the natural form of your body. Follow three basic rules:

1. Keep the waistline at the waist. Avoid having your waistband directly under the bosom or at your hips.
2. Avoid huge puffy sleeves, which make the upper arms look enormous.
3. Avoid frills, pleats, or gathers that distort your neck, breasts, arms, legs, or thighs.

You're better off draping a sheet over your head and tying it at your waist than wearing these silly styles.

The history of fashion shows a continuing conflict between modesty and exhibitionism. Avoid both extremes. Certain fashions enhance the body's contours. Select those that accentuate the natural form, such as low-rise jeans.

3. Color

Your goal in selecting clothing is to enhance your appeal to men. Don't hide your female attributes with confusing patterns. If the material has a busy print, the man isn't curious about the body tucked under the clothing. If there are too many distracting items, it will take too much effort for the man to "figure" out the body contours. He'll assume you don't want to be noticed. He'll turn his attention to others.

Basic colors are usually best. But avoid pink unless the style is very sophisticated. Pink often connotes that the wearer is a girl, not a woman. Wear clothing that preferably has a solid color, or at least has a small print or vertical stripes that don't detract from the contours of your body.

4. Fabrics

Choose a fabric that is soft to the touch and transmits some body warmth. Most natural fabrics and some artificial fabrics will do this. Above all, avoid rough, scratchy materials.

5. Undergarments

Wear comfortable undergarments that follow your body's lines, including thongs and matched bra-and-panty sets. Tight undergarments such as corsets and girdles are a misery of the past. If you own any such instruments of torture, toss them out! No matter how large a woman you are, you're more appealing if your body is unconstricted and natural. If you're bound up in girdles, you look like you're in a body cast or brace. Even if you do look ten pounds thinner, these garments are not effective in attracting men.

6. Shirts and Blouses

Your blouse should draw attention to your breasts and their cleavage, but not be revealing. Wear a pullover or a shirt-type blouse or a blouse with buttons in front. These tops hint at easy access to your breasts even if they aren't the slightest bit revealing. T-shirts are great. It doesn't take much male imagination to know that in less than five seconds, these shirts are off over your head. When you select a blouse, choose one that has an open neckline and a small collar. Let the man fantasize.

7. Skirts

Wear skirts that are on the short side, but still within the normal range in your community. If you're sufficiently thin, consider wearing a skirt that hugs your sexy body contours. If you aren't model-thin, wear skirts that loosely outline your body and appear easy to lift. Pleats, stiff materials, uneven hemlines, and other devices distort the body to sexlessness. Consider wearing skirts that button up the front to stir the man's imagination.

8. Pants

Men generally prefer to see women in skirts or dresses, not slacks. If you do wear slacks, be sure that they're a solid color. Slacks should span the entire length of your legs. Avoid plaids and pleats. Men like women in jeans because they're snug, outline the body, and represent casualness and comfort.

9. Shorts

Men do like shorts on women. Short shorts are especially appealing, but be sure that they're within the social norms of your community before you wear them in public.

Your shorts should fit relatively snugly, yet provide you with enough range of movement for your active life. Avoid pleats, even when pleats are in style; they distort your figure. As always, select a solid color, not a busy pattern.

10. Swimsuits

You don't need a bikini—or bikini figure—to lure men. But if you do wear a bikini, a solid color is usually best. Be sure the top and bottom match. Make sure your bikini isn't too skimpy. Stir the man's imagination but do not satisfy his curiosity. One-piece swimsuits are attractive, too. Don't go to the other extreme by wearing a bathing suit with a skirt or ruffles that hide your figure.

11. Shoes

Your legs look more attractive to men if you wear shoes with heels. A slight lift accentuates the calves and creates graceful leg lines. Wear shoes that slip off easily—this will incite the man's imagination. Avoid high heels that are so high, you look awkward when you walk or run. Clumsiness isn't sexy.

12. Panty Hose

Garters are sexual aids or props, not items of clothing. When you wear hose, make sure they reach high on the thighs. The last thing you want is an elastic stocking band interrupting the male's imagination as his eyes glide up your leg. Colors close to your flesh tones are often preferable, but black net hose are often sexier for special occasions.

13. Hair

The sexiest part of a woman is her face, especially if it's framed by attractive hair. Your hairstyle should make a man want to touch your hair, to run his fingers through it, even if you're not giving him permission to touch it just yet. It's "touchability" that attracts most men.

Still, you needn't have beautiful hair or spend much time on your hair to succeed with men. Most women will do better with men if they fuss less. Cleanliness and softness are the keys. Here are some specific guidelines:

> ➤ Avoid extreme styles—unless you're looking for a man who's an extremist.
> ➤ Avoid hairstyles that are too short. Here's a rule of thumb that really is a rule of thumb: Have hair at least as long as your thumb, curled or uncurled.
> ➤ If you do use hair products, avoid hair sprays, gels, and mousses that are smelly or sticky or make your hair stiff.
> ➤ Make sure your hair looks soft to the touch, not brittle.
> ➤ Once your hair starts to turn gray, the right hair coloring can be a real beauty enhancer. Most younger men don't like gray hair, because it generally makes a woman look older. If you color your hair, be consistent. Don't show your roots.
> ➤ Men love to see a woman's hair. Never wear a hat indoors. Don't wear a hat outdoors unless you have to because of the weather.

➤ Don't wear curlers when you're with your man.

➤ Avoid frizzy perms.

➤ Get rid of those split ends.

➤ Get yourself a hairdo that's fun for him to fondle. Keep your hair free of snarls and knots. Avoid fancy hairdos.

14. Jewelry

A man envisions gliding his hands or lips over the woman's neck, arms, or hands. Men view sharp objects as barriers, whether these objects are gold, silver, or seashells. Are you looking to meet new men, or are you looking to strengthen your present relationship? Your answer to this question should determine the way you wear jewelry, and even the jewelry you wear.

A man looks at your jewelry—or lack of it—as a sign of your availability. In particular, he will glance at your hands. If he sees even one ring, he may assume you're not available.

The age-old custom of a man giving an engagement ring and a wedding ring to his woman has a present-day purpose. These rings are designed as barriers to intimidate other men. The single most common mistake widows make is not taking off their wedding rings if they are now seeking to date.

If you are still looking for the man of your choice, avoid rings until you find him. A man views every ring you wear as a commitment ring, given by some other man with whom you have a relationship. You may have bought the ring yourself, or your ring may have been your grandmother's, but the man you are hoping to meet does not know its origin. Keep your heirlooms in the vault, not on your fingers.

Your watch or bracelet is the only jewelry you should wear on your hands or arms if you are questing for a mate. But men generally dislike the noise that bracelets make. Avoid bracelets with sharp edges or those that would scratch a man who's caressing you.

Wearing jewelry is appropriate on some occasions. If you're

invited to a gala event where all that glitters is gold, you'd feel out of place wearing only your functional watch.

A necklace is best if it hints at your sexuality. Consider a plunging necklace with larger jewels in the center that anchor the necklace near your cleavage. You'll do better wearing one attractive necklace that enhances your cleavage than wearing a few different and dissimilar necklaces that distract from your female form. Avoid wearing a necklace that is tight around your neck. It may appear unfriendly to the man, as well as uncomfortable for you.

Avoid wearing a pendant that looks like a locket, especially a locket shaped like a heart. Men will figure you're in a relationship already.

Avoid wearing visible religious symbols unless you want to attract a man who shares the religious belief that the symbol connotes.

Avoid sharp earrings. A man might envision himself nibbling at your earlobes or hugging you, and you don't want to distract him from these thoughts.

Don't wear your jewelry on dates at the beach, while watching a football game, or at a picnic, or at similar casual events. If you wear jewelry then, a man might view you as too materialistic. Save your jewelry for more dressy occasions.

Diamonds often are not a girl's best friend when it comes to attracting men. Perhaps they are even her worst enemy! Never wear diamonds in such a way that a man could think you are committed to someone else. You might be better off wearing other gems.

Junk jewelry is just that, junk. Junk is cute on a young teenager. If you use jewelry, wear the real thing or nothing at all.

15. Nails

Forget about growing long fingernails. Long nails may impress other women, but they don't appeal to men. Men view long fingernails as "claws." Long nails indicate that the woman is unwilling to participate in household tasks or enjoy recreational activities. Keep your nails at a working length and without jagged edges. Long fingernails dampen a man's image of your touching his sexy body parts.

16. Makeup

One major error that many women make is the excessive and incorrect use of makeup. You're better off with no makeup than with the wrong makeup.

The sexiest part of a woman is her face. If you're looking to attract men, your face needs to look kissable. This doesn't mean that you're giving a stranger permission to kiss you, but you do want him to think about kissing you. Unless you select your makeup very carefully, it will hinder rather than enhance your appeal.

Don't surround your eyes by circles of color. If your eye makeup is obvious to a man, you're using too much.

Minimize your use of face powder. Men are not eager to rub cheeks with a woman who is caked with powder or foundation. Men don't enjoy that taste.

Careful use of makeup may keep you from looking too young and sexless, or too old and haggard. Older women generally need more makeup or color enhancements than younger women, so your makeup strategy may need to be updated from time to time.

17. Perfume

Excessive use of perfume makes a woman less desirable. It is better to wear no perfume at all than to use too much. If you like wearing a scent, choose a cologne or toilet water rather than a perfume for a more pleasant aftereffect.

Don't expect a man to share your interest in perfumes. He is highly unlikely to know or care about brand names.

18. Teeth

You kiss with your lips, of course, but you also kiss with your teeth. Make sure your teeth are appealing:

➤ Brush after every meal. Use dental floss or a toothpick if necessary to remove particles between your teeth. Do this privately, not in public!

➤ Good dental care is essential, but the man isn't interested in your cavities, caps, and fillings unless he's a dentist. Make sure that your teeth look natural. Avoid looking like a mine that has been excavated for gold and silver. Since your man doesn't care about your dental work, don't make it a conversation topic.

➤ If you're missing teeth, get false teeth. Missing teeth are a definite turn-off.

➤ Bad breath is a turn-off. Refresh your breath often throughout the day.

19. Overweight?

Are you worried about your weight? Then here is some good news. You don't need thin thighs to marry the man of your choice. A few extra pounds will rarely cost you a relationship. In fact, you are much more likely to lose the man by extreme dieting, especially if the diet involves self-denial. Don't be overly conscious of your weight, or you'll make him conscious of it.

Don't delay your quest for a mate with the excuse that you must diet. You don't have to choose between love and food. Nothing is gained by trying to starve yourself.

If you weigh 20 percent more than the standard weight for your height, however, you will lose a few men. Your losses will climb dramatically if you weigh 50 percent over the standard weight for your height. If your weight is double the standard, it will likely be difficult to find anyone to date. Of course, if you're truly obese, weight reduction is in order. Make weight reduction your priority if you are shorter than five feet tall and weigh more than three hundred pounds. More than dating is at stake here.

20. Eyeglasses

Are you wearing glasses to see or to be seen? A carefully chosen pair of glasses will make you more attractive. How you deal with people depends upon how you see them. If your vision is inadequate, you will be losing out. Nobody wants to date someone who fumbles and stumbles.

Contact lenses are not necessarily preferable to glasses. Here are some hints for selecting eyeglasses:

➤ Select the thinnest lens that gives you the optical correction you require.
➤ Avoid glasses that are too trendy, stylish, or extreme.
➤ The man must be able to make eye contact with you, so avoid reflecting glasses, prism glasses, and other glasses that hide your eyes.

chapter 3

Meeting Men

Now that you're dressing in a friendly manner, it's time to start meeting men. Your ideal mate is scarcer than one in a hundred, and probably closer to one in a thousand, so you need to meet many men to find the man of your choice. You're ready to begin this initial step in your manhunt.

TAKING THE INITIATIVE

The man you are seeking can be yours, but only if you take the initiative. Unless you can find diamonds in the street and pearls in your chowder, don't expect the man of your dreams to appear on your doorstep without any effort on your part.

Assume for a moment that you're considering becoming a gold prospector. You would formulate ideas as to what you need to carry out your mission: basic equipment, personal effort and energy, and, of course, a location where you're likely to find gold. No matter how ignorant you are about prospecting, you certainly wouldn't expect to find gold nuggets in your front yard, nor would you ever imagine that someone will ring your doorbell and say, "I understand that you are seeking gold. Here, I've brought you some."

Finding a mate is similar to panning for gold. Both take effort! Society may have you convinced that there will be some magic moment in your future when you'll meet and marry your ideal prince, all by chance! You may believe that the only requirement on your part is patience, and that you should sit back and wait. With this philosophy, all that will happen to you is menopause and old age. Wake up! No man is going to knock at your door and ask, "Does a nice girl live here? I'd like to marry her."

Men have little courage when it comes to women. This explains why Plain Jane, who takes the initiative, is married and you are daydreaming.

Begin with Eye Contact

One of the first steps in meeting a man is making eye contact. Eye contact is crucial in showing a man that you find him worth meeting. Still, while he may be very desirable, try not to stare or gawk.

Keep on Smiling

Another first step in meeting a man is to smile. Your smile is one of your most attractive attributes. Smiling is special, and part of the whole process of saying hello. It's fun, it's easy to do, and, after all, smiles don't wear out. So keep smiling.

Have a Tourist Attitude

Have you ever noticed that it's easier to meet people when you travel than it is when you're home? Acting like a tourist can help you overcome shyness and meet more interesting men. I have a friend who's a travel buff. When she's away from home, she doesn't hesitate to approach any man for directions, general conversation, or guidance. She can ask a man for an explanation of his customs, his ideals, or his culture. When she's a foreigner in a foreign land, she is not influenced by her culture's illogical taboos.

She isn't questing for marriage during her travels, so she feels at ease in her conversations. She treats every man as a book from which she can extract a unique story. This technique works so well that she meets incredibly desirable and available men—men who seem unapproachable to the women in that country.

At home, however, she was tongue-tied. She thought about the ease with which she initiated conversations abroad, and decided that if her tourist personality loosened her tongue, she should be a "tourist" at home. Now she carries a camera and tries to look "touristy," which gives her the license to approach anyone with any excuse. Men respond quite positively to her initiative.

Saying Hello

The first thing you must do is say hello to every man where you live, where you work, where you shop, where you conduct your business, and where you go for recreation. Greet every man you are reasonably sure is not a danger to you.

Many women cannot easily approach a man and say, "You look like an interesting person, and I would enjoy talking to you!" Society has taught us not to approach men we might like. We are pressured to respect social barriers and use "proper" channels to meet men, so we remain in our own social circles, with little chance of meeting new men.

For some women, the most difficult phase of a relationship is the beginning, the initial creation of interest. You need some courage to create interest and initiate the contact. Go ahead— you can do it! Most men will respond favorably to your friendliness and will start a conversation or give you the chance to begin one. The key is as simple as a smile and the word *hello*.

First Impressions

First impressions are the strongest—and are often irreversible. A man is most likely to view you in his mind as he did when you first met.

Act at all times as if you believe in yourself. Don't act like a loser or otherwise allow yourself to exhibit any feelings of inadequacy. Present yourself as a winner, and soon you'll become one. You don't know what man is waiting around the corner to meet you, or is observing you from afar. Act as if you're meeting the man of your choice.

After You Say Hello

Your initial hello and conversation with a man should take ten to fifteen minutes. Ask him about himself. If he has recently arrived in your city, for instance, you could use questions such as these:

➤ What brought you to this city?
➤ What have you enjoyed the most about being here?
➤ How different is this city from where you come from?
➤ How long do you plan to live here?
➤ Has it been easy to make new friends?
➤ What interesting places have you found in this city?
➤ How are you spending your free time?
➤ How often do you visit home?
➤ How often do friends visit from home?
➤ How does this city differ from what you expected?

Ask questions that require an explanation rather than a one-word answer. Make it easy for the man to tell you about himself—because in this first conversation, he is likely to tell you how unique or different he thinks he is from other men. He will probably disclose ten to twenty facts about himself in this brief conversation, facts you must try to remember if you are interested in him.

Look for any fact or combination of facts that you feel makes him different from other men. If you find him interesting, tell him so, and tell him why. Then indicate how he can see you again. Say, "I usually have lunch here on Tuesdays and Fridays. Maybe we can talk again next Friday." If you don't find him interesting, say good-bye. You need to expand your horizons and meet as many men as you can, but you also need to begin the weeding-out process as soon as possible.

Exchanging Telephone Numbers

When a man asks you for your telephone number, ask him for his as well. Don't give your number to a man who won't give you his. And, to be even more cautious, give him just your cell number or work number—home numbers come into play when you feel comfortable with each other. Once you have his number, use it. Verify that the number is really his before you date him.

If you are not comfortable calling up a man, remember this call is only a "polite" gesture to acknowledge that indeed it was a mutual pleasure to meet. Many men have bad memories of women giving them wrong numbers so as to never be found. The more the man likes you upon meeting, the surer he must be that:

1. you are who you say you are.
2. he can contact you at the numbers you provided him.
3. you'd welcome a phone call from him.

A two-minute call to say that you were glad you met, and that you would like to have a cup of coffee with him since you found him interesting, makes it easier for the man to take the next step in dating. The days of waiting for a man to make the first move are long gone!

Begin your dating relationship in the daytime and in public places. Delay the more intimate encounters until you are more sure of the man and your relationship with him.

NETWORKING

Networking can greatly increase the number of men you meet and the chance of meeting the right fellow. Keep track of other single women you know, especially those women who are not attracted to—and therefore would not be competing for—the men you want. Your female friends can be strong allies in your quest for a mate. Here are three benefits you can get from strengthening these female friendships:

1. *Ego boosting.* Your morale and self-esteem can be damaged by the outside world, but your female friends who are very supportive can boost your confidence.

2. *Strategies.* Discuss specific strategies and techniques with your friends. Many of the skills you will learn later in this book, such as interviewing and conditioning, require thought and practice. Your friends can be very helpful.

3. *Information exchange.* When you meet a man and determine that he's not for you, save his telephone number. Write down some information about him on the back of his card. Now you are prepared to swap numbers with the other women in your network.

You also can benefit from networking with single men who are not prospective mates. These men may be willing to introduce you to their friends—and they may be interested in meeting yours.

BE APPROACHABLE

If you are approachable, you can meet men everywhere. A man is really a large-sized boy looking for someone to talk to. Chances are, if you have a smile on your face, he'll start a conversation anywhere, but your best bet is to be in a place where he can meet you again. Some men will return to the same place they've seen you just in the hope of meeting you.

Some women meet men easily, while others don't. Some women go to parties, clubs, and social activities, and don't meet men. Other women can't go to the supermarket without receiving flirtatious looks or being approached again and again. The difference is that one woman is approachable and the other is not.

Many men surround you in your daily life, but you probably don't even know they exist. Some of these men may be looking at you with great longing, but they're afraid to speak to you unless you look friendly. The more approachable you are, the more successful you'll be at meeting men.

The Man's Fear of Rejection

Men have little courage when it comes to approaching the women they truly want. A man will much more readily approach a woman he finds slightly attractive than one he is enthralled by; he has less to lose if the former rejects him. That's why those ordinary women are married and Wonderful You is single and daydreaming.

Men may be courageous on the battlefield and ambitious in business, but they fear female rejection. Yes, they may be avoiding you because they fear you'll reject them. A man's sexual image of himself, including his desirability as a male, forms shortly after he reaches puberty, and this self-image rarely changes. Even twenty years later, after years of career success, the man's self-image remains the same, and most men have a very poor one when it comes to approaching women. The man you see as a tall, handsome stranger is a shriveling fourteen-year-old inside, worried about blemishes on his face, his cracking voice, and rejection by you.

In your teenage years, if you were at a school event and no boy asked you to dance, you may have felt overlooked. But think of the boy with a sensitive ego who had to ask the girl to dance with hundreds of people watching. If the girl refused his invitation, he wasn't just overlooked. He was rejected. The rejection was no doubt devastating to him because it felt like public humiliation.

What did that young boy do to avoid the embarrassment of rejection? He approached only those girls who looked friendly and who were happy to return his glances. When it comes to meeting women, men still behave as they did when they were boys: They approach women whom they believe won't reject them.

Friendliness and Approachability

Treat every man as worthy of a friendly hello. This attitude will minimize male fears of rejection. Just smiling a warm hello at every man, whether he's your paper boy or your lawyer, will give you the reputation of being a friendly person and make it easier for men to approach and meet you.

This doesn't mean that you should offer sexual invitations and longing looks. You can achieve approachability just by smiling, exchanging the civilities of the day, and offering one thought of recognition—say, "It's always pleasant to see you and say hello."

Do so with every man in your life. You'll develop a habit of making men happy to see you, and you'll become more comfortable with male friendliness. As a result, eligible men will speak to you, including men you thought were unavailable or didn't exist in your world.

You may fear that your friendly reputation or your high approachability will attract men, but not the superior man you want. Don't worry. Your ideal man views himself as superior to other men. For this reason, he's not going to approach you if he's unsure of a friendly reception. After all, he's afraid that if you reject him, people will find out, and it will be a public humiliation. If the man of your choice sees that you extend the courtesies of the day to all men, however, he will dash over, believing that he can impress you.

Let's imagine that you are at a party and a handsome stranger named Carl catches your eye. You want to dance with him. When Al comes over and asks you for a dance, you say no because you want to keep yourself free for Carl. When Bill comes over, you turn him down for the same reason. Do you honestly think that Carl, who has seen you reject two men, is going to run the risk of being rejected, too? Emphatically *no!* But if you had accepted Al's and Bill's invitations, Carl might have mustered the courage to come over, too.

PRECONDITIONS

What if you are especially selective? Suppose you have decided that you want a man who has a certain profession, recreational activity, ethnic background, or religious faith. First, recognize that your preconditions will severely limit the number of men you can meet. Since you will undoubtedly be looking for various emotional and physical characteristics as well, your ideal mate may be even *scarcer* than the one in a thousand mentioned earlier.

If you are not dissuaded, then go to places where the men meet your requirements, whether this place is a professional organization, sports center, or ethnic club. Once you're at that place or event, though, be friendly to everyone. No matter what group you have selected to begin your quest for a mate, never act like a snob within that group. Smile and say hello to all the men—and the women too.

WHERE TO MEET MEN

Men generally have images of the types of places they expect their wives to patronize and the types of activities they expect their wives to engage in. By extension, they have similar expectations about the places to meet their future wives. Go where the men are, but find places that don't work against you.

Bars

Bars are rarely a suitable place to meet men. Many people act falsely in bars, and inebriation changes their behavior further still. (Pubs that serve food are a different matter, though.) Men are unlikely to marry women they meet in bars unless they want a wife who is a bar patron. Meet in a sophisticated singles bar if you must, but skip the rest. Of course, what is crucial is your and your man's own moral code about alcohol consumption.

Whatever the case, though, if you are meeting men in bars, meet them after work, not later in the evening. Otherwise, you might spend many hours with someone who won't even remember you the next day.

Churches

A church can be a suitable meeting ground, but only if you are very religious and you insist on marrying someone of the same faith. Be sure to tell your pastor you're looking. Otherwise, you'll do better at your place of worship if it's open to the public.

Twenty Successful Meeting Places

Bars and churches are some of the most common meeting places. Since they aren't the best places to find your future husband, where should you look? Some places on this list may surprise you:

1. *Your job.* Start with the men at work, but don't stop there. Meet men through your job, as well as on your job, including suppliers and customers. The key to meeting men is having access to them and taking the initiative.

2. *Bookstores.* It's so much easier to discover a man's interests if you meet him at a bookstore. Many bookstores serve coffee and provide you with the chance to sit and read. You're likely to meet more thoughtful men at the bookstore. Don't be too quiet and shy—a bookstore is not a library. Ask him what books he recommends, and offer your advice. Besides, men who are looking for interesting women know to look in bookstores.

3. *Supermarkets.* Shop in the early evening, when most single men are shopping. Ask for help if you can't reach an item on the top shelf, but never act clumsy. Better yet, give *him* the chance to ask for *your* assistance in selecting produce.

4. *Laundromats.* Evenings and weekends are the best. Bring extra bleach and fabric softener—you'd be surprised what men forget when they do the laundry! Bring soft drinks, too, since Laundromats are steamy and rarely air-conditioned. If you see an interesting-looking man, ask him for change to use the machines, then offer a soda after you receive the change.

5. *Libraries.* If there isn't a convenient bookstore nearby, try the library. In a large library, you can pick your section— and men—very carefully. Sit down and meet men at a leisurely pace. Try the magazine section—it's the least formal, and the most conducive to conversation. Try specialized libraries if you want to meet a man interested in a particular specialty.

6. *Bowling alleys.* Bowling has many advantages over other sports: It's year-round, all-weather, and inexpensive. Besides, it's easier to socialize at a bowling alley than at most other athletic facilities: Players are seated right next to strangers, and skill levels are completely mixed. As a result, it's easy to meet someone new.

7. *Gym.* Get flexibility and strength—and a man—at your gym. Try "You look fit—how long have you been coming here?" as an icebreaker.

8. *Travel.* Be a tourist and meet men wherever you go. Try places that get few tourists; you'll get more attention there.

9. *Doctors' waiting rooms.* When you go to a doctor's office or the hospital, it's easy to meet men in the waiting room. "How long have you been a patient of the doctor?" or "How long is the wait?" might make a good opener. But forget this technique if you are going to an obstetrician or gynecologist!

10. *Civic or political groups.* Civic associations and political parties can involve major commitments of time and effort, but they do give you the chance to meet many interesting men.

11. *School.* School is a good opportunity place for meeting men, even if you're past the usual school age. Try night school enrichment classes. Teach a class rather than take one if you can. Select topics that interest you and also appeal to men.

12. *Parties.* It's hard for a party to be active but relatively quiet at the same time, but that's the best type of parties for meeting men. Avoid the loud music, limit the alcohol, and you're off to a good start.

13. *Affinity clubs.* Put your activity or hobby to use in meeting men. If you collect stamps or coins, or comic books or records, you can meet men who share your interests. If you're more of an elitist, try an airline club, a country club, or the yacht club.

14. *Coffeehouse.* There's more brewing in the coffeehouse than coffee.

15. *Sports groups.* Sports groups usually have more male than female members. If you like softball, boating, tennis, or golf, you have a great opportunity for meeting men.

16. *Shopping.* Go to shops that have a lot of men, including places that sell electronic equipment, sporting goods, or tools.

17. *Charities.* You can meet kind and generous men if you invite them to join you in charitable work. Help make sure benefit performances run smoothly, or participate in other fund-raising activities.

18. *Public events.* Go where the action is—the mayor's swearing-in ceremony, a political debate, or a public hearing about a controversial issue. Be an active participant whenever you can, and ask questions.

19. *Restaurants.* Yes, you *can* meet men in restaurants. Besides, you have to eat anyway. Ask a patron what he thinks about a particular item on the menu. Breakfast is a good time to meet men. You and he'll be rushed, but you'll have the chance to meet the next day or exchange phone numbers. The counter offers great proximity.

20. *Public transportation.* Don't ignore your travel companions, especially if you see them on a daily basis.

Go Solo

Many women go husband hunting with a female friend. This strategy is often a mistake, because a man generally does not approach a woman unless she is alone. You may prefer the companionship of a female friend over going to places solo, but a man may be too shy to approach two women together, even if he's very interested in meeting you. If you're with a female friend and a man does approach you, you run the risk of his developing an interest in your friend instead of you. If you do set off to meet men with another woman, separate once you arrive at your destination.

LOVE AT WORK

I've said that your job is one of the twenty best places to meet men. Men, however, do not usually pursue the women they work with. Instead, they typically view their co-workers, colleagues, and other female business contacts as off-limits when it comes to dating and mating. Why are they missing some good opportunities to meet truly desirable women? Let's look at the personal and business reasons.

Personal Reasons—Fear of Rejection

Men dread rejection from a woman. The higher a man is in his company, the more true this statement becomes. As a result, men need privacy when they ask a woman for a date. A man needs assurance that if the woman rejects him, the rejection will not become public knowledge. If a woman gossips to her friends about a man she rejected, other men may hear this. They'll be afraid to approach her, and she has lost these potential dates.

Men often feel that they don't truly have access to women they meet in a work context. They don't feel free to come over and ask a woman out, especially when she works in a different department or is employed by a separate company. Suppose he is visiting the woman where she works and someone comes over to him and says, "What are you doing over here in the widgits department?" He will be too embarrassed to answer, not because he is ashamed of the woman, but because he fears that her overt rejection of him would become company gossip.

If a man is reluctant to contact you at work, he may try to call you at home or by cell phone. If he can't find your number or it's unlisted, you'll never know of his interest in you.

The problem is worse if you're an executive. Many men would like to meet you, and some might want to marry you, but how many of them could get through your secretary? Because men are often awkward in approaching women they truly want, and they are easily intimidated, your efficient secretary may have weeded out their calls. Or did she take them herself?

A man may try to minimize any potential ego bruising by using a business meeting as an excuse to see you. Then, if you reject him, he won't take the rejection quite so personally. Perhaps he calls you to say that there are a few additional details on a contract he would like to work out with you. You remember him, don't you, the fellow you told to "check it with the legal department"? Or perhaps he told you he wanted your idea about a new product, but you were too busy to give him the time of day. Be on the lookout for male co-workers who interact with you more often than they really have a business excuse for. They may be interested in *you!*

Business Reasons—The Corporate Chaperone

Businesses exert enormous pressures that make it even harder for men to approach women through the workplace. These are four problems that men face:

1. An extension of the incest taboo: Dating a female co-worker is, in a sense, like dating his sister.
2. Company rules against fraternization and nepotism.
3. Laws against sexual harassment: The man fears that his pursuit may be subject to legal challenge.
4. The general attitude that a man who has time for woman chasing at work isn't doing his job.

The corporation, in its role of "Big Brother," has become the corporate chaperone, keeping people apart. What's a woman to do? Can you find love at work? Don't expect men to be upfront about their desires. They are intimidated by women and afraid of the corporate chaperone. Watch them maneuver and manipulate so that they can spend time with women who interest them. You *can* meet a man on the job or through your job, but the man faces too many obstacles in taking the initiative. *You* have to take the initiative and meet him. Join him at coffee break.

Selecting an Occupation

Some occupations lead to more marriage opportunities than do others, but I hope you don't select an occupation just for that purpose. You usually won't need to change occupations to meet more and better men, but you may find it worthwhile to change employers or to change job functions where you now work. Here are some basic guidelines:

> ➤ Have access to men in a way that makes it easy to say hello.
> ➤ Create opportunities to talk with men and find out about them.
> ➤ Exchange information that matters to the man and to you.
> ➤ Be seen as approachable and friendly.
> ➤ Show concern with the man's comfort.

What follows are twenty occupations you may never have considered that can increase your chances of meeting eligible men.

1. *Investment Adviser.* You won't meet large numbers of men as an investment adviser, but the men you meet will be among the most successful. You can get to know them readily when they seek investment advice because they'll reveal their goals and dreams as well as their finances.

2. *Men's shoes sales.* Since every man must buy his own shoes, you can meet large numbers of men by selling them. Then, when you meet a man, ask him about his shoes to open up a conversation about his lifestyle. Ask him where his old shoes

have been. Then ask him where his new shoes will be going. Or sell the kinds of men's clothing that he'd have to try on. Otherwise, your purchasers may be other women.

3. *Accountant.* If you're shy and looking for a man who is private, this may be the occupation for you. Similarly, consider being a tax auditor. You will have access to any man, even the most difficult to meet. Equally important, you will have his attention when you meet him.

4. *Automobile sales.* Most men enjoy buying a car. If you are a knowledgeable saleswoman, you can add to the fun they'll have trying out and selecting a car. You'll be meeting on a positive note because these men will share their enthusiasm with you.

5. *Attorney.* Protect the man from the outside world and win him over.

6. *Medical equipment sales or pharmaceutical rep.* You'll have access to the medical community that the laywoman doesn't. You'll meet large numbers of doctors and technicians, and you can impress them with your knowledge instead of standing in awe of them.

7. *Barber.* You'll be meeting many men. You'll start out with physical closeness and have the opportunity to talk.

8. *Politician.* You'll meet many of the most interesting men in the community. Since you can work on legislation on a variety of topics, you'll have easy access to almost everyone.

9. *Security guard.* You'll have power, and access to many men. You can stop whomever you want and ask him questions!

10. *Bank officer.* If you're watching over a man's money or helping him borrow in a financial crisis, he'll feel friendly and grateful. Your job also gives you access to much information about him that other women can merely wonder about.

11. *Sports reporter.* You'll be meeting many men in excellent physical shape. Besides, they'll have a great excuse to tell you about themselves. Be a reporter, not a fan, and they'll take you seriously.

12. *Heavy equipment sales and repair.* Men love heavy equipment such as haulers, cranes, loaders, and forklifts. You'll have the inside track to their inner thoughts.

13. *Fire/rescue.* Some men enjoy being rescued. After all, when injured they revert to childish helplessness.

14. *Zoning inspector.* Meet business owners, and observe their operations. You'll have the chance to ask probing questions.

15. *Investigator.* You'll clearly have the inside track to knowing men as they are and what they're portraying themselves to be.

16. *Computer sales.* Even today, many more men than women buy computers. It's your chance to see what his needs are.

17. *Office design.* This is your opportunity to ask him about his plans for the future. Then you can ask him about his likes and dislikes and his plans for the present.

18. *Web design.* Here's your chance to design his unique and special Web site. You may be the first to recognize how unique and special he is, too.

19. *Dispatcher.* You can tell him where to go—and how far.

20. *Chauffeur.* You'll take him to where he needs to go. Ask him why he's going there while you tell him about restaurants and events en route.

DATING WEB SITES

Here are three approaches you can use to meet men through dating Web sites:

1. Include your profile in the personal database, enabling men to select you.
2. Sort through files of available men, selecting those you'd be interested in meeting.
3. Do both, including your own profile *and* sorting through files of available men.

Dating Web sites typically insist that real names and addresses remain confidential; the parties need not meet unless both decide to do so. Extreme caution is the order of the day.

This is an example of the information dating Web sites should contain, for you and for your man:

PHOTOGRAPH—HEAD SHOT

OBJECTIVE FACTS

➤ Gender
➤ Date of birth
➤ Height
➤ Weight
➤ Hair color
➤ Eye color

➤ Ethnicity
➤ Religion
➤ Residence location
➤ Location where grew up
➤ Marital status
➤ Children
➤ Education
➤ Occupation

EVALUATIVE FACTS

➤ Body type
➤ Income level
➤ Smoking
➤ Drinking
➤ Political viewpoint
➤ More about me

ATTITUDES AND PREFERENCES

➤ Personality traits
➤ Favorite activities
➤ Favorite cuisine
➤ Favorite music
➤ Favorite reading matter
➤ Favorite leisure activities
➤ Physical activities

ABOUT YOU

➤ Your goals
➤ Ideal first date

In seeking a potential mate, many individuals try to be all-inclusive when it comes to attitudes and preferences. Credibility is key here. Perhaps a person may genuinely enjoy ice skating and water polo and fourteen other sports. Perhaps this person really is both open-minded and spiritual, and has seventeen more dynamic personality traits. Perhaps this person enjoys motorcycling and wine tasting together with sixteen other favorite activities. Perhaps not.

Here are some guidelines for meeting your Internet date:

➢ Meet only in public the first few times.
➢ Ask him for details about himself you can verify.
➢ Check his story with people you know or trust.

If you're looking for a dating Web site, get on the Internet superhighway with www.RomanceRoad.com to take advantage of a two-month free offer, starting with Time Warner's publication of this book.

SPEED DATING EVENTS

Speed dating helps you begin your relationships faster. It's a meeting and initial cross-interview with a number of fellows all at once. It's similar to a job fair, where prospective employees meet with a number of employers, or to a college fair, where prospective students meet with university representatives. Speed dating organizers advertise these events from time to time in Web sites or newspapers, so be alert.

Speed dating events are an updated version of the "mixer," but without music and dancing. The organizer sets up the events, advertises to attract participants of both sexes, runs the events, and collects revenue from the participants. Each participant provides the organizer with her (or his) basic information, pays a fee to attend the event, and, of course, becomes part of the organizer's database for promoting future speed dating events.

The speed date facilitator typically sets up a number of events, often organized by age range and geographic area and then by like-minded interest groups—whether by profession, religion, fetish, or quirk. A speed dating event is typically organized to have the same number of participants from each sex—often a relatively small number of people, such as twenty-four women and twenty-four men—who then meet in a structured environment.

Speed dating events typically take place in a restaurant, but without food and beverage service. One group at the event (men or women) stays in place while the individuals from the other move from table to table. Each woman meets each man during the two-hour event, typically for five minutes each.

The old-fashioned mixer emphasized agility and dancing ability, but speed dating emphasizes a different skill set—good looks and rapid verbal communication, as well as being memorable and having a strong memory. The conversations often degenerate to "lines" and glibness. You'll have perhaps two minutes to be memorable, and you'll have significant competition. Perhaps all men will remember is your physical attributes.

When embarking upon a speed dating event, consider your dating goal—is it to secure the maximum number of dates for fun and frolic or is it to meet someone you might like to pursue into marriage? You might find that men are more interested in dates for fun and frolic and less interested in marriage than you are.

With all that, though, speed dating has a fundamental flaw. Ask yourself: Would you prefer to reject a man or give him the chance to reject you? Many of us, men and women, will reject a potential partner too quickly if we fear that we'll be rejected. In short, speed dating often causes women and men to say no to each other too quickly. Five minutes with a man who doesn't want you can be the harshest rejection you've ever felt.

chapter 4

Dating

Conduct your dates with marriage in mind. *Conversation* should be the operative word in this stage of your marriage quest. Have fun with your friends or classmates. Enjoy movies, concerts, sporting events, or the theater with your co-workers and family— but not with a man you are interested in.

Diversions make it harder for you to get to know your date. Diversion driven dating can wait until your relationship with a man is secure.

Instead, take the time to converse with the man you're interested in. Do this whether you're going out for coffee, having lunch at a family restaurant, or enjoying a summertime picnic lunch in the park. Dating is your prime opportunity to evaluate the men you meet and develop relationships with them.

Create the opportunity for a man to spend time with you at little or no cost. At first, he'll invest either his money or his emotions in you, but not both. You want his emotions! Let him have a great time talking freely about himself. The man will seek you out again just to spend time with you.

You should, by now, be starting to meet a wide variety of men. You'll have many more dating opportunities as you go forward into your quest.

PLANNING YOUR DATES

Your dates will be more successful if *you* plan a variety of activities. Don't rely on your men to be creative. If they are, that's strictly a plus.

Surprisingly, few women bother to plan their dates. Provide a variety of activities to give him new experiences and change his daily routine. Even if the man is reluctant at first to do something different, he will eventually find it very enjoyable. You'll be getting the man accustomed to spending his free time with you. Even if another woman entices your fellow away from you for a while, he will miss the variety you provided him. He might be initially curious about her, but he should return to you with enthusiasm.

You needn't find exotic activities. Check the newspaper for events and be courageous enough to suggest what to do and where to go. Be sure the man can easily afford the activity, or pick up the tab yourself. Be sure as well that he has the proper clothing or equipment to participate in the activity. You wouldn't want him to go bowling in his business suit!

Take the effort to gather information that would make the date more interesting. Tailor each outing for the man. Your competitors aren't putting in this effort, so he'll enjoy his time with you more.

Dating Activities

If you live in a large city or in a tourist town, you can easily achieve variety in activities you suggest. Here are some attractions you might consider, depending on where you live and the weather:

> ➤ Boat rides
> ➤ Places of historical interest

➤ Bookstores
➤ Zoo
➤ City hall
➤ Church events
➤ Museum
➤ A personally prepared walking tour
➤ Classes of mutual interest

Even if you live in a small town, you should be able to come up with fun activities at a minimum cost, weather permitting:

➤ Picnics
➤ Bicycle riding
➤ Fishing
➤ Sunbathing
➤ Photography
➤ Walking in the park

Here are some more interesting things you might be able to do on a date:

➤ Visit the oldest building in town.
➤ Go to an ethnic restaurant where the food is new to you and him.
➤ See your city from its tallest buildings.
➤ Take a guided tour of your own city.
➤ Visit a newspaper office to see its operations.
➤ Attend a lecture on a subject that interests both of you.
➤ Go to a TV station and become part of a live audience.
➤ Go bargain hunting at a flea market, antiques shop, or garage sale.
➤ Visit a manufacturing plant that offers a tour.
➤ Go to a railroad museum, old train station, or automobile museum.

Remember, the key to dating is conversation. Make sure your activities provide plenty of things to talk about.

DATING MANNERS

Your man is always judging you on your manners, whether you realize it or not. He may not even be conscious of it, but he remembers and evaluates the way you act toward him and others.

Just as you need to discover his true moral code, you need to discover his true sense of manners and decorum. His culture and experience are good clues.

Many men, especially those who are older, believe they should be chivalrous. They'll expect the woman (whoops—lady) to be served first—even if her food gets cold. If the man you want in marriage believes in chivalry, let him know that you expect him to be chivalrous. You may need to go along with formalities that seem stuffy or silly, such as waiting for him to pull out your chair from the table, but the sacrifice may be worthwhile for the right man. Be careful, however, that he doesn't treat you too much like a prim and proper lady and not enough like a woman who has sexual needs.

These days, dating manners are still important, but are much less sex-differentiated than those in the past. Your fellow should treat you with kindness and expect the same from you. Here are specific manners guides to successful dating.

Telephone Manners

➤ Call him. The days of a woman not calling a man are long gone.

➤ Call him at convenient hours. Try not to disturb him at his office.

➤ Keep him on the line only if the conversation is thought provoking or he's emoting. Have something interesting to say or make the call short and sweet.

➤ If someone calls you while you're with your man, ask the caller to call back. If your relationship is serious, let him know who's on the line by mentioning the caller's name. These actions let him know that he's special.

> Whenever he calls you, greet him warmly by name. Let him know that you're happy to hear from him.

> If you're at his home, don't answer his phone unless he suggests that you do so.

With His Parents

> Address his parents as Mr. and Mrs. until they invite you to use less formal names. Don't use familiar expressions such as "Pops" when speaking to his father!

> His parents are *always* on his side no matter what they might say or do, so *never* complain about their son to them.

> Chances are that his parents are much older than you. Don't expect to be waited on hand and foot when visiting with them. Offer your assistance instead.

> Don't assume that his parents have the same values as you. Avoid making comments that might upset them.

> His parents may want to discuss their interests and tell their stories. Be a good listener. Encourage them to talk about themselves.

> Keep your shoes on unless they remove theirs.

> Don't wander around their house without permission or intrude on their territory.

> Avoid using vulgar words in front of his parents.

> Tell his parents, if you believe it, that they've raised a wonderful son.

> Tell them, if it's true, that you hope to see them again soon.

Dating Courtesies and Economics

> Be considerate of the man's finances when he takes you out, just as you would with a female friend or relative.

- ➤ If he forgets his wallet, offer to pay expenses or lend him money for the date.
- ➤ At a restaurant, when he is paying, order the least expensive item that appeals to you.
- ➤ Be willing to pay for a significant portion of your dates.
- ➤ Invite him to restaurants as your guest, or offer to cook for him.
- ➤ Never act helpless. Even if he finds helplessness cute when you first meet—and most men don't—he'll later hold it against you when it comes to marriage.
- ➤ If you are with your man and you meet someone you know, introduce him proudly.
- ➤ Avoid ethnic slurs, political diatribes, and extreme religious statements.
- ➤ Avoid using vulgar language with your man, especially if he hasn't used the word first.
- ➤Don't entice him sexually unless you're seeking a sexual encounter.

At His Home

- ➤ Respect his privacy. Leave cabinets, drawers, and closets shut until he invites you to open them.
- ➤ When you use his kitchen or bathroom, straighten up after yourself.
- ➤ If you're hungry while at his home, don't raid his refrigerator without his permission, but do expect him to offer his hospitality.
- ➤ Tidy up his home just a bit. This suggests that you care about creating a nice home environment.
- ➤ Use your own hairbrush, comb, or other toiletries. Don't borrow his.
- ➤ Keep clean. This is the sexiest thing you can do for yourself.
- ➤ Show interest in any trophies or awards he displays.

➤ If you use anything at his home, put it back in the same place.

➤ Compliment his home where you see he has expended effort.

➤ Don't make decorating suggestions until you know him well.

➤ Leave his mail alone, whether he's opened it or not.

At Your Home

➤ Tell your fellow where the restroom is. Many men end a date earlier than the woman desires because they're too shy to use the bathroom.

➤ Serve tasty refreshments.

➤ Provide a comfortable seat and a reasonably neat area for talking.

➤ Play music in the background. Vary the music from country to classical to jazz, because music creates moods. Later in your relationship, you'll need music to change moods.

➤ When your relationship with him progresses, tell your fellow that he's welcome to make himself at home. In particular, invite him to raid your refrigerator anytime he wants.

➤ Your attitude about your home should be that it is a fortress against the world. When the fellow is there with you, encourage him to share this feeling.

➤ If you cook for him, make sure you prepare what he likes! Don't try to impress him with gourmet dishes he won't enjoy.

➤ When your relationship is exclusive, give him free access to your home by giving him a key.

➤ Share your goods freely. Let him use your phone, stereo, TV, and other equipment.

➤ Designate special places for him—his place at the table, a certain chair, his own drawer, and so on.

➤ If he wants to help you with household jobs, let him. The more effort he puts into your "nest," the more emotion he is investing in you.

TOUCH HIM, AND ACCEPT HIS TOUCH

Human beings crave touch. Part of your bonding process will be touching the man you want and accepting his touch of you. The touching process begins shortly after you've met the man and before you've selected him to be your life's long-term partner. I'm talking about touching here, just touching, not fondling or engaging in sexual activity. A sexual relationship takes place much later in the relationship.

There are many ways to touch and be touched: a handshake, a pat on the back, a hug, an arm around another's shoulder, a stroke of the arm. All this touching takes place when it's consensual. Think back to your youth, and to how your family members and close friends treated you. Didn't they give you hugs and affectionate touches? Now think back to the young boys in your life. Didn't they get the same type of touching from their family members? Extend such touching to the man in your life.

Men generally touch other men in a manner that's different from how they touch women. These differences are apparent, even when sex is not a consideration. Young men jab, punch, shove, and horse around with one another as a means of physical contact. Women rarely touch in this manner. The men in your life seek a pat on the back and an arm around their shoulders. Men don't normally provide arm strokes to one another. Women, in contrast, do stroke the arms of men they're fond of. Simply by stroking a man's arm, you'll be fulfilling his need to be touched. As your relationship with this fellow progresses, it's time to touch. It's time for holding hands and a hug.

KISSING

When you and your fellow first begin your dating relationship, kiss him as each date ends, and expect him to kiss you. Kissing is an art. Early in the relationship, your kiss should be more than a perfunctory peck on the cheek, but less than passionate. Save your passions until bonding develops and you view him as a potential mate.

WHAT TO WEAR

Once you've established a dating relationship with a man, you expect him to dress in a manner that pleases you. Do the same for him. Chances are, you might eventually be selecting his clothes, so let him participate in selecting yours. You have some outfits that appeal to him and some that don't. Wear what he likes when you're together and expect the same from him.

Dress as a couple. Your clothing and his should match, not clash, whenever possible. Don't wear dots when he's wearing stripes. Better yet, follow the same color scheme if you can, especially when you dress casually. You have more clothing options than he does, so be more flexible.

Don't neglect a neat appearance once you're dating him on a regular basis. Appearance remains important.

COOKING FOR HIM

If you spend the night with a man, whether in your home or his, be prepared to help him get breakfast the next morning. As a rule of thumb, if you don't think enough of a man to make breakfast for him, you shouldn't have spent the night in the first place.

Make eating together a special event for the two of you. And if he enjoys the kitchen, try cooking something together—that can be the most fun of all! If you know what he likes, consider being his special chef. If he likes to cook, let him, even if he leaves a mess. But always minimize the time you spend in the kitchen if it means he's alone.

PLANNING FOR YOUR NEXT DATE

If you want to see the man again, don't forget to plan for your next date before this date ends. Otherwise, good night may mean good-bye.

chapter 5

Selecting the Right Man

Once you've started dating a particular man, how do you know if he is that special one who is your ideal mate? How do you find out what you need to know about him? How do you know he will fall in love with you? Apply this basic principle to find out what you need to know: "Interview" him for the job of husband before you "audition" for the role of wife.

KNOWING WHAT YOU WANT

You shop for food, clothing, and more. Are you putting as much effort into selecting a man? Let's assume you've been invited to a special event, and are planning to buy a new outfit for the occasion. You'd need to know your dress size, your shoe size, and the colors and styles that flatter you. You'd view yourself in the mirror to evaluate your overall appearance. You might even ask close friends or relatives for opinions on your selections. You'd know the price you'd be willing to pay for the outfit. Now ask yourself whether you've put in the same effort into your marriage selection!

Can you imagine how difficult it would be to buy your outfit if the shop had no standard sizes? Imagine having to try on every outfit in a shop just to find one that fits! Well, going out in the mating world without knowing exactly what you want can be just as chaotic as shopping without knowing your sizes, needs, budget, or style preference. "One size fits all" is a myth, at least when it comes to mate selection!

I'm not suggesting that there is a meat market—or "meet" market—where you can go to find men, or that men are for "sale." Unfortunately, men are not gathered and conveniently labeled at designated shopping areas! But men are virtually everywhere. Your "shopping list" helps you promptly recognize a man who could interest you.

Preparing for Your Search

Unless you're too choosy, the more specific you are in defining your ideal mate, the more efficient your search will be. You may have never concretely defined or spoken openly and frankly about all you seek in a mate. Be bold about what you want.

Let's assume your ideal mate is one in a hundred. If you were to spend six months seeing each wrong person, you'd need fifty years to find an ideal mate. Instead, let me help you become more efficient in your "husband shopping."

So how do you start shopping for a husband? Start by creating a shopping list of what is crucial to you in selecting a mate. Recognize what you want—and don't want—in a man, then spend effort only on those men who meet your requirements. Have your own shopping list. Don't borrow your friend's list unless you plan to borrow her husband, too.

Who's the Buyer?

You wouldn't say to a clerk, "Please just take my money and give me whatever outfit you have." You are the customer with something of value to exchange for whatever goods you like! Likewise, you aren't the seller in your marriage quest, but the buyer. You have much to offer a potential mate. You don't need to sell yourself. Be choosy rather than waiting to be chosen.

Are You Too Choosy?

Suppose you need a man who's caring, such as a social worker, teacher, or nurse. But then suppose you need a man who's on a rapid path to economic success. If you seek a caring person who is acquiring great wealth, you're seeking a combination that's unrealistic. It's akin to being a large-sized woman wanting to fit into a small size.

Don't be unrealistically choosy. There should be a number of men who meet your requirements. From these men, you should find a man you love and who loves you. Focus only on factors that are crucial to your well-being, what you truly want and need. As a further reality check, if you've never even met a man who measured up to all your criteria, then you're asking for the impossible. Time to rethink what is or isn't essential for you. Modify your standards now if no one has ever met them.

INTERVIEWING HIM FOR THE JOB OF HUSBAND

Choosing a man for marriage requires considerable effort. You cannot sift men through giant colanders, but you can sift them through your life by learning about them. Then you can pick and choose among the best.

Begin by having casual conversations with your man before working in an interview. But begin your interview as soon as possible during the dating relationship. After all, one of your priorities is to use your time wisely.

Caution is needed here. Don't turn your dates into inquisitions! Instead, use your time wisely to discover what your fellow is really like. If you ask him questions about himself, there won't be lulls in conversation, and you won't have the pressure of thinking of some brilliant and impressive things to say. He'll enjoy sharing his thoughts with you.

Know the man before you dare love him. A lasting love is based on knowledge, not assumptions and wishes. If to know him is to love him, your love will be real.

Benefits from Interviewing Him

Don't kiss the frogs to find your prince. It's no fun to kiss a frog, not to mention a waste of your time and risky to your health. A better strategy is to let men tell you about themselves. Cut through the morass by interviewing the men you meet in such a way that they'll fully reveal themselves to you, so you can eliminate the unsuitable ones quickly. Then, when you have selected the man of your choice, encourage him to continue talking. Let him *talk* his way into love with you (a technique I'll discuss in the next chapter).

Once you become skillful in conducting these interviews, the man may not realize he is being interviewed. But even if he does, he'll still tell you about himself. Men love talking about themselves. Many men will seek you out if they think you're a good listener. What does being a "good listener" entail? Paying attention to what your fellow is saying, remembering the highlights of what he said, and asking him probing questions. If you don't want to expend so much effort, this man is wrong for you. Move on.

The interview techniques described in this chapter are designed to enable you to discover a man's virtues and his faults. A man will be eager to tell you about his virtues, but reluctant to discuss his faults. With a little nudging, you'll know both. Then, when you've made your tentative selection of your future mate, continue open listening to gain the information you need to praise and criticize him effectively, win his love, gain his respect, and demonstrate to him that you are the right mate for him—all techniques you'll learn later in this book.

SCREENING IN, SCREENING OUT

Let's start the interview process with three basics of screening:

1. Determine if there is something special or unique about the man. Is he worth more than a ten-minute conversation? If not, eliminate him right away.
2. Determine if his values and goals are compatible with yours. Could you live with him over a long period of time? If not, stop wasting your time.
3. Determine if the way he relates to people is compatible with your expectations and requirements and meets your emotional needs.

Let's look closely at these three facets of the screening process.

1. Discovering His Uniqueness

The first step in the interview process is to determine if there is something special, different, unique, or exciting about the man from your perspective. This process is your initial screening of potential mates. Most men are sufficiently interesting to merit your further attention beyond this initial screening. The key is to ask him about himself. Don't focus on yourself quite yet. You'll have plenty of time to tell him about you later—after you've decided that he's worth it.

2. Values and Goals

Ascertain the man's values and goals early in the dating relationship to determine if he is a potential mate for you. But before you use the selection criteria presented on the next page, discover your own values and goals by answering these questions yourself.

Take the time to seriously reflect on your answers, so that you can compare them with his.

This comparison will demonstrate crucial aspects of your mutual compatibility. Your responses to these questions need not be identical to his, but they do need to be compatible. If he wants two children and you want four, it will probably be a compromisable difference. But it will not work out between you if one of you does not want children and the other does. Look for full compatibility on any issue that is crucial to you, and look for general compatibility on the noncrucial items. Insist on full compatibility if the value or goal is a "zenith"—one that absolutely cannot be compromised.

Here are some questions that you can ask him to help start eliciting information concerning his values and goals:

> Do you believe in heaven and hell?
> Do you believe you will come back to earth in the future as another being? If so, what do you expect to be? When do you expect this event to occur?
> How often would you like to go on vacation?
> What holidays do you celebrate and with whom?
> Do you prefer living in the city or country? Why?
> Would you like to visit a foreign country? Which one?
> Would you ever give up your citizenship? Under what circumstances?
> What are your attitudes concerning abortion?
> What would your dream house be like?
> What are your personal commandments?
> What is your attitude toward minorities?
> What are your attitudes concerning capital punishment?

3. His Interpersonal Relations

Ask the man questions that pertain to the way he treats other people and is treated by them. He will probably treat you in a similar manner and expect comparable treatment from you. Then determine if his interpersonal relations—the ways in which he interacts with people—are compatible with how you'd want him to treat your family and friends. These are just some of the questions you can ask to elicit information:

> Do you believe that you've enjoyed life more than your friends?
> When in your life were you most popular?
> How did you meet your best friend?
> Do you generally trust your co-workers?
> Have you or would you ever run for an elected office? Did you win?
> What's the most money you've ever borrowed from anyone? The most you've ever loaned?
> When in your life did you feel most alone? Most supported?
> How many children would you like to have? Why?
> What makes you angry? What about women makes you angry?
> What events of your life were more fun in retrospect than at the actual moments you experienced them?

THE LISTENING PROFESSIONS

The interview skills you can use as part of the mate selection process draw upon the listening patterns of four professions: law, journalism, the clergy, and psychiatry. People who succeed in these professions have mastered the skills necessary to become professional listeners. If you want to increase your success and status with the opposite sex, you need to master these skills and use them to your advantage. Let's take a closer look at the listening skills required for the first two professions (we'll look at the latter two in the next chapter) and how they'll help you learn about your man.

Law

Lawyers elicit facts from their own clients and examine witnesses in depositions and at trial. Thus, one of the most important legal skills is getting witnesses to testify. The lawyer controls the witness by asking specific questions and urging that the questions be answered. Then the lawyer asks related questions to determine if the answers are consistent. Ask questions and cross-examine your fellow, when necessary, to check his answers for consistency.

Journalism

The investigative reporter asks thoughtful but probing questions to elicit information. Each answer usually leads to another question. Reporters want the whole story in a logical sequence, and they don't stop until they get it. Make sure that when a man tells a story you get the *whole* story, including his motivations.

If He Hesitates to Talk to You

Men who are in the listening professions sometimes hesitate to speak freely because they know the consequences. The journalist knows that if he talks, he's bound to say something he doesn't want to see in print. The lawyer knows that if she speaks freely, she may give information to the other side that could be used against her or her client. Members of the clergy know that they may inadvertently "confess" and lose some of their holy image. The psychologist or psychiatrist risks falling in love with the listener.

If your man is in a listening profession, or just plain reticent, it will take slightly more effort on your part to get him in the habit of talking freely. You'll have to reinforce that the reason you are asking questions is because you find him so interesting and unique. Your purpose is not to expose his secrets or cause him any harm. Be persistent and ask questions about a time or place that are not threatening. Ask about his vacation, teenage years, opinions on popular issues, far-into-the-future issues (such as what he thinks the common mode of transportation will be in a hundred years or the electronic devices humankind will have at its disposal). When a man starts to feel comfortable talking—and he will—you'll know you have earned his trust.

BASIC INTERVIEWING RULES

The key to good communication is not talking, but listening. We are often willing to talk, but we are rarely willing to listen. You have heard the expression, *Talk is cheap.* Well, the opposite side of the coin is, *Listening is expensive.* People in the listening professions earn significant sums and acquire important influential positions just by listening.

The interview process utilizes probing questions, active listening, and analysis of the man's responses. Catalog and process the information so you can use it later. These listening strategies have nothing to do with meekness, for you are not a passive listener. Instead, these techniques will change you from a casual listener to a professional listener.

Interviewing is more difficult than it appears, but you *can* acquire this skill. These are the five basic rules to conducting a successful interview:

1. Direct the conversation to key topic areas.
2. Let him talk.
3. Show interest and remember what he says.
4. Do not censor his comments.
5. Do not criticize or ridicule him during the interview.

Let's look at these five basic rules.

1. Conversational Direction

Direct the man's conversation to your areas of interest. Discover what he is truly like as a person by asking him questions about his attitudes, values, and experiences. If you're afraid that you may seem too nosy by bringing up a subject out of the blue, you can tell him that you read an article in a newspaper, had a dream, were asked your thoughts on the matter, or heard the issue raised on a talk show. Discuss such sensitive issues as abortion, premarital contracts, whose career has priority, and investment decisions when the occasion fits.

2. Let Him Talk

Listen to his revelations instead of reciting yours. You're better off knowing him before you reveal yourself. Avoid interrupting him, and, in fact, encourage him to fill in the details in what he says. A nudge such as "Is there more?" or "Is that all?" can often give you precious tidbits.

3. Show Interest and Remember What He Says

Show him with body language and verbal cues that you want to know about him. Look at him attentively during the conversations as if you were paid to listen; don't putter around. Maintain eye contact, and encourage him to talk by listening carefully. Focus the conversation on him. When there's a lull, ask him about another facet of his life.

Remember what he reveals about himself. The knowledge you gather will be your key to deciding whether he is a prospective mate for you, and will help you develop your personal strategy.

4. Avoid Censorship

Do not censor his conversation by refusing to listen to a particular topic. (Though later in this chapter, I'll examine some exceptions to the no-censorship rule.)

5. Avoid Criticism and Ridicule

Do not criticize him during the interview phase of the relationship. If you criticize a man at this point for exposing his thoughts, feelings, or experiences, he may become anxious and silent, or tailor his remarks to avoid offending you. Keep your opinions, ideas, and attitudes to yourself at this time, so that you can discover him as he really is. If you still want him after he's revealed himself, you'll have plenty of opportunities to express your thoughts.

HOW TO ASK QUESTIONS

You will be far more successful in eliciting information from your man if you know how to ask questions, and if you know what questions to ask. Your questions should often begin with the word *why*. Avoid asking questions that could be answered with a simple yes or no.

For maximum benefit, ask questions in the most neutral language that you can, so that the man does not know your views. If he does know what your attitudes are, he may pretend to have the same views in order to win your favor. You lose control of the relationship if you disclose your views too soon. "Do you like cats?" is neutral. "You like cats, don't you?" is not. *Don't you* indicates the answer you want.

Ask questions in a specific context. You can use newspapers, magazines, television programs, or books to provide this context:

There are always plenty of current events involving politics, religion, sex, money, and other things that matter. Use these events as "props" to elicit his attitudes. His stories are filled with indications of who the man thinks he is, who he wants to be, how others see him, and who he really is. Discover him as a public person, as a private person, and as a potential mate.

As you listen to a man tell you about his values and his interpersonal relations, you can form a true picture of his personality. Picture what life with him would be like. Focus on money, sex, zeniths, energy, and what he wants in a mate, and see if you like the picture he's painting with his words.

THE LISTENING PROCESS

The listening process is both open and active. Both of these facets are essential if you are to realize your objectives.

You will be practicing "open" listening by letting him talk freely about himself. No rules! Let the man complete his train of thought and discuss any topic for as long as he's on a roll. As you listen to the man telling about himself, don't be totally silent. Encourage him to continue talking.

You'll be practicing active listening by making such comments as "That's interesting, tell me more" or "I enjoy hearing about you." If necessary, prod him gently by making a comment, going back to his most recent revelation.

The listening process is active rather than passive because you should evaluate, categorize, and remember what you hear. Then use this material to elicit and cross-check further information by paying close attention to what the man is saying. Be an active listener. If you don't want to listen to what your man is saying, that's a clear sign that you should be moving on.

As a listener, you need to be empathetic. *Empathetic* does not mean "sympathetic." To be empathetic, say "I understand" to let him know you understand the depth of his feelings. Don't show sympathy—that you feel sorry for him—unless he's relating an event that involves sadness for him.

Also, as a listener, you should be disinterested, but not uninterested; in other words, you should be objective where possible, but you should not be bored. If you are quickly bored, move on. He's not the right person for you.

THE INTERVIEWING CHRONOLOGY: PAST—FUTURE—PRESENT

To discover what made a man who he is today, ask him first about his past, then about his plans and expectations for the future, and finally about the present. People are usually reluctant to talk about their present attitudes and actions. They fear that the information they give you could be used against them.

People will discuss their past and future more readily than the present because the information doesn't necessarily apply to their present lives. For example, at the early stage of your relationship, your fellow could find it highly inappropriate for you to ask him what he earns now, but he would undoubtedly be willing to tell you how much he earned in his first job and what he plans to earn ten years from now.

Start the interview by asking your man to tell you about his childhood. As he continues, encourage him as far as you can. If you are an effective interviewer, you'll have a little boy before you, reliving the little boy he was.

Then ask the man about his youth, particularly the years in which he was in school. Use gentle, probing, and pleasant questions. Ask him when he first owned a car, when he started dating, who were his female and male friends, what attracted him to particular girls, what sports he enjoyed, and what he liked best and least about school, work, and home life.

Allow the man to communicate whatever he likes. Wait patiently and quietly until he begins to tell you all. When he brings the conversation to the present, he's placing his trust in you. Then you can ask questions about his current life.

As your man is recalling events of the past, portions of his reminiscence will not be as interesting to you as they are to him because he is emoting as if the events are happening now instead of just being remembered. The longer he continues reliving the past, however, the closer your relationship will become. Encourage him to tell you more. Let him know you share his joys and sorrows.

The more a man talks to you about his past, the more likely it is he will speak about his future. Ask him about changes in his life, what caused them, whether his priorities shifted (and if so, why or when), the goals he has reached, and his new goals. Ask him where he wants to be and what he wants to do at some time in the future.

Be sure to raise—not avoid—controversial topics. As a youngster, you may have been told not to discuss sex, politics, religion, or money. That rule makes sense, if at all, only when you are dealing with casual acquaintances. These four topics—sex, politics, money, and religion—are among the most crucial when you are interviewing men to choose your future husband. Ask questions about anything and everything that is important to you. Then listen to and evaluate his answers.

Painful Memories Lead to Positive Results

I remember my twelfth birthday and the joy it brought. My dad, a government employee, had saved up to buy me a special bike that he gave me that day. It was just the right size, and I enjoyed it thoroughly. But someone stole the bike just three days later. A painful memory even now.

One of the techniques I espouse is active listening, asking probing questions and doing so without revealing your thoughts. Over my years as a lawyer, I've had occasion to use the active listening mode with more than a thousand people. It can be very difficult to keep your own thoughts out of the active listening process, and, like you, I faced situations where I wanted to blurt out my true thoughts full force.

On two occasions (years apart) when I encouraged people to talk about themselves, two individuals revealed that they had once stolen a bike. The phrase *eternal damnation* crossed my mind, but I followed the technique of active listening instead.

I asked questions: "What type of bike was it?" "What did you do with the bike?" and finally, "How did you feel about stealing a bike?" Because I asked neutral questions, I got more thorough responses. The first bike stealer revealed that he had experienced a "rush" from stealing his first bike and is now stealing cars for a living. The second thief became remorseful and a churchgoer because of his misdeed. Without active listening, I would have treated both people the same.

WHAT YOU'LL LEARN ABOUT HIM

When you are contemplating marriage to a particular man, evaluate him as a prospective husband. Don't be ashamed about making this evaluation, for he is also evaluating you as a prospective spouse.

The evaluation process should be conscious and rational, based on real facts and emotions, but all too often it is unconscious and irrational, as well as haphazard and incomplete. If you want to marry the man of your choice, you need to enhance your ability to evaluate men realistically.

Here's what you can expect to learn about a man when you interview him thoroughly:

1. His self-image
2. His personality traits
3. His acceptance by others
4. His threshold for praise and criticism

5. His pride in his achievements
6. His philosophy of life

This information is absolutely essential. You'll need to understand where he is coming from so that you can lead him where you want to go.

1. His Self-Image

Discover your fellow's self-image as a man, reflected in how desirable he views himself to women. His self-image most often formed and jelled during his teenage years. If he was popular, he may expect you to fawn over him as teenage girls did, even if he's long past his prime. If he was unpopular, he likely lacks the confidence to assert himself and he expects you to reject him.

2. His Personality Traits

Discover your fellow's personality traits, including his attitudes toward the world in general and toward women in particular. From listening to his early experiences, you can ascertain his attitudes toward sex, money, religion, family life, and his profession by his past actions, rather than what he says.

> ➤ Is he considerate to others, or rude to them?
> ➤ Is he social or antisocial; a "party animal" or a loner?
> ➤ Does he follow popular trends or does he confront popular opinions?
> ➤ Does he have social graces, or is he clumsy in conversation?
> ➤ Does he expect too little from others or too much?
> ➤ Does he entertain others or does he expect to be entertained?
> ➤ Does he provide many compliments, or does he criticize you more than he compliments you?

3. His Acceptance by Others

Be alert to areas in which your fellow must excel to compensate for inadequacies he once felt, or for things he once lacked. Listen to his revelations carefully to determine how he thinks others view him. You will discover his self-perceived reputation and determine whether it is deserved. This is a beginning point for the information about him that you should know:

> ➤ What people does he like or dislike, and why?
> ➤ How does he want to be viewed by the world, and why?
> ➤ How would his family and friends describe him?

4. His Threshold for Praise and Criticism

Look for his threshold for criticism—how much criticism brings on fight and how much more brings on flight. You also should be able to determine how much praise he needs to feel good about himself, and how much he accepts before disbelieving its source. Praise and criticism are so important that I've devoted the whole of chapter 8 to this topic.

5. His Pride in His Achievements

A man is proud of his achievements, even if the outside world diminishes them. He wants to tell someone about his struggles and triumphs, and wants acknowledgment for his less dramatic accomplishments. If you want to succeed with a man, become his confidante and share his joys and sorrows. If you disparage his achievements or don't want to be his confidante, he is not your ideal mate. Move on!

6. His Philosophy of Life

Discuss the future and "what if" situations such as these to understand his true philosophy of life:

> If you had a million dollars, how would you spend it?
> If you could date anyone in the world, who would you choose and why?
> If you could travel anywhere in the world, where would you go?
> If you were president, what would you accomplish?
> If you were a judge, how would you view your cases?
> If you were in charge of education, what would you want taught in our schools?

Vary the mental imagery you provide your man. Just as he wouldn't read the same novel over and over again, vary the subject matter you discuss with him, so he's not bored talking with you. Consider his mind a fresh canvas. Paint upon it any picture you wish using words. Carry your fellow through imaginative journeys. His responses to your imagined scenarios will give you insight into what motivates him, and help you appreciate him.

MONEY

A person's attitude toward money is one of the more crucial components in marriage because money touches all aspects of life. If you and your spouse don't hold similar attitudes about money, you're almost certain to face a turbulent marriage.

Listen carefully to what the man says when it comes to earning, spending, saving, and financial responsibilities. He is likely to expect you to handle *your* money in the same way he handles his. Concentrate on the following areas to learn about a man's financial attitudes.

Survival Anxiety

What amount of money does he require to feel financially comfortable? Some men are happy with a steady job paying a modest income. Others need more significant sums in the bank before they lose "survival anxiety," the feeling that they are vulnerable to economic disaster.

Spending Versus Saving

It's important to determine what sacrifices the man will make to keep his money. These are some of the questions you should be able to answer:

➤ Would he prefer to live in a posh palace or in a simple home and bank the dollar difference?

➤ Does he wear ordinary, and unstylish clothes rather than purchase new items?

➤ Does he pass up favorite foods because they are too expensive?

➤ Does he drive an old car because newer cars cost money?

➤ Does he refuse to buy anything until it has a bargain price?

➤ Is he unwilling to spend a little more just for aesthetics or just to save time?

➤ Does price motivate everything he buys, from the cheapest self-service gasoline to the wine he drinks?

➤ Does he go to a movie only at the matinee price and take his own candy?

➤ Does he prefer being cold in winter to paying higher heating bills?

➤ Does he insist on sending his children to public schools rather than private ones because public schools are free?

➤ Is he resentful of paying for items such as the barber, lawn mowing, or maid service?

If the man resents paying for his luxuries, he will also resent paying for yours. He may even resent your paying for these things yourself.

Or maybe the situation is the opposite. Perhaps you are frugal and you resent a man who spends money for show or for comfort, especially if the funds are yours or they're joint funds. Determine if you and he have compatible attitudes.

Spending Priorities

Ask the man what he would do if he suddenly inherited a significant amount—pick the amount that would be appropriate under the circumstances. Don't accept his flip answer. Instead, ask him to give some serious thought to what he says. His answer will indicate his financial priorities.

> ➤ Would he purchase a snappy wardrobe?
> ➤ Would he quit work for several years and play, or attend school, or work on a pet project?
> ➤ Would he invest or save all or part of the money?
> ➤ Would he purchase gifts for people who are close to him?
> ➤ Would he set up his own business?
> ➤ Would he give any of it to charity?
> ➤ Would he treat the amount as too small to bother with?

Family Versus Money

Learn how he divides his time between earning money and being with his family:

> ➤ Will your potential mate prefer to spend time with the family rather than earn more money?
> ➤ What are his plans for career and children?
> ➤ Will he work fourteen hours a day, travel a great deal, and leave you to raise the kids primarily by yourself?
> ➤ Does he prefer that you work or care for the children in their tender years—or both?
> ➤ Does he plan to work until he falls apart or take a premature early retirement?

Real Survival

Discover what your man's behavior would be if hard times hit by asking him how he behaved in the past when money was scarce. You can expect the same attitudes if hard times return. If his family was poor or provided him with little money during his teens, chances are he will always have a "survival" mentality and will be very conservative with his money. If, on the other hand, his parents were well off and he learned to take money for granted, he may spend more lavishly as a result.

SEX DRIVE

Sex is a crucial aspect of marriage. It's important to know his sex drive and compare it to yours, since sex is such an important basic need. If the man's sex drive is higher than yours, he is likely to do other things for you to secure the privilege of rolling over in bed and finding convenient sex. On the other hand, if your sex drive is greater, you will have to cater to him to obtain the sexual activity you'll need. A man who has a high sex drive has a higher tolerance for your foibles, tends to be more generous, and generally is kinder to women than is one with a low sex drive. The operative word is *need*. A woman with a low sex drive can demand more, whether that's help with the housework, tolerance for her personality quirks, or greater decision power. If he needs more sex, he'll do more to achieve it and sacrifice more for it.

Ideally, the two of you should have equal sexual needs, but no two people are perfectly matched. The person with the lesser need for sex usually becomes the boss because the other person must relinquish power for sex. The person with the higher sex drive may try to have a pleasing personality or undertake activities that the spouse might favor in the hope of getting sexual favors.

ZENITHS AND AVERSIONS

Zeniths are the goals that cannot be ignored or even compromised successfully. They often include money, power, prestige, fame, and accomplishment. You or your fellow might have different zeniths that will clash, ruining your relationship.

If your zeniths and your fellow's are in conflict, move on and find someone else. If you interfere with a man's pursuit of his zeniths, or if he agrees to ignore them, your marriage may be doomed from the start. Do not abandon your zeniths, either.

You also need to discover his aversions—those things he dislikes intensely. The two of you do not need to have the same aversions. Be certain, though, that your aversions are not inconsistent, and do not conflict with the other person's zeniths.

Zeniths and aversions you should have in common include attitudes toward money, careers, lifestyles, prestige, and fame. The probability of marital success is high if you have compatible attitudes toward money and sex, and share zeniths and aversions.

Position, Power, and Prestige

A man often wants to equal and preferably surpass the other men and women in his family in position, power, and prestige. If his father is the boss of his business, the son is likely to view himself as a future boss of that business. His family may have a tradition that he plans to continue of being lawyers, pilots, military officers, politicians, doctors, accountants, musicians, forest rangers, police officers, actors, or undertakers. It's important for you to ascertain whether he and his family have such expectations, and whether you support them. He may not be able to marry you if you cost him his family dignity by objecting to his occupation.

Know early into your relationship what your man's values and traditions are. You are fortunate if you have access to his family, because then you can observe how he reacts to their expectations.

If his family grooms him to be a politician, they'll expect you to be a politician's wife, and will turn against you if you refuse that role.

If your man was raised in an orphanage or foster home or suffered youthful deprivations, he may need an exalted position in life to feel important and will do what is necessary to achieve it, expecting your full support.

Religion

Religion is a zenith for some men. If a man believes that he was born to be saved, and that life in the hereafter is what life here is all about, he isn't going to stay married to a nonbeliever unless he feels it's his duty to "save" this woman. If you're a nonbeliever and he gives up on saving you, you're out of the marriage. If your fellow had a religious upbringing, but now has no formal religion, he may still follow his childhood customs. He may expect certain types of behavior from his wife and future family because of his religious upbringing. Know what he expects from them before you marry him.

Physical Attributes

Most men have an idea of what they want in a woman physically, just as you are likely to know what you want in a man. Be aware that some men have inflexible physical standards for their mate. This is sad but true. Some men like legs, others like breasts, and others like fannies. If your male likes a big bust, and it is his zenith to enjoy big bosoms, he is going to be unhappy with you physically if you have small breasts. You should know what his standards are when you interview him. Then try to discover if his rigid requirements have caused him to break up with women in the past. If you are far from his ideal, his displeasure will eventually surface. Before too long, he's likely to go elsewhere to find what he misses in you.

Practical Knowledge

Many men expect a woman they might marry to have practical knowledge in a family setting. Even if he fails to articulate this concept, a man may expect his wife to have the same knowledge as his mother did. You too will then need practical knowledge to make your life together enjoyable and reduce the likelihood of hassles. Here are some examples of what a man might expect from a woman:

- ➤ To be a prudent purchaser in the household setting
- ➤ To replace a broken toilet seat
- ➤ To paint a room
- ➤ To work household equipment
- ➤ To interact with your children's teachers
- ➤ To know something about nutrition, portions, and calories
- ➤ To know his clothing sizes, and to help purchase and care for his clothing
- ➤ To know who the local vendors are, and how to reach them
- ➤ To complain to a vendor if an order is wrong
- ➤ To care for a pet

Education

Some men want an educated woman. This is particularly true if his family values education. If you don't have a formal education comparable to that of his female relatives, prepare yourself for further schooling or serious home studies, or realize that you and he may have conflicting zeniths.

Lifestyle

Your man is a creature of habit. You can change some of his habits but not others. Determine what facets of his everyday life he won't change. Observe his preferences for foods, entertainment, hobbies, friends, political views, pets, personal hygiene, and dress style, and try to find out which of these preferences are intractable.

ENERGY LEVELS

People have different energy levels, and this difference is critical. You'll be better prepared if you know his energy levels and yours. Ideally, energy levels between spouses should be similar. Otherwise, the more energetic person may come to consider the partner a dud. The person having less energy may consider the other hyperactive. This energy to which I'm referring is a force that relates to physical activities other than sex—dishwashing, exercise, food preparation, walking, and so on.

Different energy levels create problems when one person wants activity but the other doesn't. The high-energy person may require little rest or sleep, and may need to be active constantly. This high-energy person usually expects his or her mate to join in activities and may interpret a refusal as a personal rejection rather than lack of stamina. This will likely create serious marital problems, including feelings of frustration, anger, alienation, and rejection, if it continues over a long period of time.

Observe your potential mate's energy level and decide if you can reach it and if he can reach yours. If your energy levels don't match, plan alternative ways for the more active person to displace excess energy. Ideally, the energetic person can join a gym or undertake projects around the house that require energy.

WHAT DOES HE WANT IN A MATE?

A man marries for several reasons, especially for good companionship, for good sex, and to secure a suitable mother for his children. But note that each man has his own value judgment of what makes a woman "good" and "suitable." When you're interested in a particular man, extract from him the criteria he is using to judge and select his future mate. Good companionship, as far as he is concerned, may consist of a fellow jogger, a gourmet cook, or a professional colleague. Find out exactly what's on his mind.

It may surprise you that what a man says he wants in a wife and what he really wants are often not the same. When you recognize his real desires, the things he actually responds to, you can treat him accordingly.

How Well Do You Know Him?

After you have spent some time interviewing the man, test yourself to determine how accurate and complete your knowledge is about him. Can you predict what his behavior would be under most circumstances? Set up imaginary situations and ask him for his reactions. See if your guesses are correct. Do you know all his zeniths? You're going to have to make the most important decisions about your relationship with him based on the knowledge you have gained from interviewing him. Make your determinations carefully and accurately by testing your predictions occasionally.

AVOID THESE CONVERSATIONS!

Four types of conversations waste your time and his: hearsay, private topics, trivia, and outrageous statements.

1. Hearsay

A man may tell you stories of other people's lives that have been told to him. These stories have little value for your purposes because they rarely reveal the man's own values and goals. These stories don't tell you about his relationships with others. Try to redirect the conversations back to *his* life. Stories that pertain to others are called "hearsay" by lawyers; this type of testimony is usually barred from use in the courtroom. Such stories have just as little value to you.

2. Private Topics

Avoid conversations that relate to your private life—the life you do not share with your man. If you're a teacher and he isn't, don't talk about your students. Don't tell him about your boss's new hairdo, or the gifts your co-worker received at her shower, or the dental problems of your aunt. In general, he won't be interested in conversations about people he doesn't know unless they're public figures. If these people are important to you and are likely to remain so, introduce them to him.

3. Trivia and Idle Chatter

Avoid trivia when you can. Consider anything to be trivial if it cannot affect your life or his. It's a bad sign if someone returns too often to trivia; usually it means that he really doesn't have other thoughts to express, he can't reveal himself to you, or he has something to hide. It's always appropriate to ask, "How does this affect your life?" to tactfully turn the conversation back to him.

4. Outrageous Statements

Censor your man's monologue when he's telling you something so outrageous that you know it isn't true. You can do this by saying that you don't believe what he says, but you find him interesting anyway. If he exaggerates his stories to the point that he can't prove them, then he'll be too embarrassed to see you again. You certainly don't want that! But even if what he says is untrue or downright outrageous, it's still valuable information for you. His exaggerations and lies indicate what is important to him and his wishful thinking. These are important clues to what his zeniths are.

AN EXAMPLE OF GOOD LISTENING

The Soviet Union was known for its secret cities. No one was allowed anywhere near these cities except Russians having high governmental credentials. The KGB and police even barred communist officials from Eastern Europe and Asia to protect their secrecy. "Shoot on sight" was the standard command, and these officials monitored their checkpoints on a constant basis.

I wouldn't have thought that such a secret city would be our headquarters for *How to Marry the Man of Your Choice* in Russia, but that's what happened. The USSR gave way to the Russian Federation. This erstwhile city lifted its "shoot on sight" order and invited me in, the first foreigner in the city. I lectured to more than a thousand scientists, engineers, and cosmonauts—all predominantly male—on brainwashing techniques (which they professed not to know) and, quite interesting, on their choice of subject—marriage techniques.

I asked the elite group why they wanted to hear about marriage strategies. One space engineer spoke for the group, saying they'd been taught how to be comrades. "You're the first who's going to teach us how to love," he replied.

A very handsome cosmonaut and his wife, a quiet and plain woman with thick glasses and a hearing aid, attended my presentation. Afterward, I asked the cosmonaut what had attracted him to his wife. "No one had ever listened to me with the intensity and interest that she did," he replied. Then I asked her how she became such a good listener. Her response makes me smile to this day: "Oh! You see, I wear these glasses because I have poor vision and am hard of hearing. When I was dating my husband, I was too vain to wear my glasses. I couldn't take my eyes off his lips for a second or I wouldn't know what he was saying. I moved very close to him and never took my eyes away."

BUT WHAT ABOUT ME?

If a man impresses you, you may want to tell him your innermost thoughts during your early dates. Wait. Do not reveal too much about yourself yet. Here are five good reasons why:

1. Don't waste effort talking about yourself until you decide the man is a suitable mate for you. There will be plenty of time to talk about yourself and express your ideas later—if he passes your interview and the relationship continues. You'll likely eliminate at least nine out of ten men you meet. Then tell your private thoughts only to the few who remain.
2. You may frighten the man away before he knows you well enough. Save some topics, including your hopes and dreams, until he has invested emotions in you.
3. If you wait until you complete the interview of the man you want, you'll then know his needs. You'll then be better able to emphasize attributes that are most important to him in a wife.
4. If you tell him about yourself too soon, you may inadvertently censor him or cause him to tailor his description of himself and his values and goals.
5. If you let him do the talking early in the relationship, he's more likely to fall in love with you. Your premature disclosures may interrupt his conversation and stop him from transferring affection to you. I'll get to that technique in the next chapter.

Be prepared to convince the man that you are the right woman for him, but don't do it yet. Wait. If you decide that you want a man for marriage, you can then prepare a "sales pitch" personally tailored to him. (More about this in chapter 12.)

chapter 6

Let Him Talk His Way into Love

Once you've interviewed and selected a man for the job of husband, the next step is to help him fall in love with you. You do this by using the "transference of affection" technique. Encourage your man to reveal to you his thoughts, feelings, and goals without any restraint. The more he shares his feelings with you, the deeper his affection for you will be. He will talk his way into love with you.

Earlier in your relationship, you wanted all the information you could find about him in order to select him. Now the focus is just on him and his transfer of feelings and love to you.

You can gain his love only if you are an empathetic listener. You'll need to invest more of your own time and emotions, so don't use this technique unless you're serious about this man.

THE TRANSFERENCE OF AFFECTION TECHNIQUE

When we reveal our thoughts, actions, ideas, or personal history to another person, we also relive the emotions attached to them. We then transfer to our listener the emotional feelings for the people and things we are describing. This transfer takes place even if these emotions have long been dormant within us.

Transference is regularly used by members of the clergy, counselors, psychiatrists, and psychologists to help control behavior and develop loyalty. Many teachers, fortune-tellers, fund-raisers, secretaries, salespeople, and other professionals also use this technique successfully. When you use this technique, you get his love and affection.

Let's take a look at two of the ways the transference technique is used in our society.

Religion

Members of the clergy have the skill to elicit confessions from their parishioners. They encourage the believer to tell all because they offer comfort or forgiveness. The parishioner gets emotional relief from unburdening, and transfers gratitude to the church.

The best-known example of transference of feelings is the Roman Catholic confessional. Once inside the confessional, a person exposes inner secrets, desires, and thoughts to an empathetic listener. "Telling all" makes the person feel important, loved, cleansed from guilt—and therefore grateful.

Psychology

Psychiatrists and psychologists use their listening skills to elicit emotional responses. They encourage their patients to talk freely about events in their lives that have emotional content, and they listen with empathy and interest. They do so by asking their patients, "How do you feel about that?"

Sigmund Freud discovered that as his female patients told him any thoughts that came into their minds and were listened to without criticism, they tended to fall hopelessly in love with him. Though Freud was not a handsome man, he sat out of his female patients' sight to prevent this. Women fell in love with him anyway, however, even though they were talking to "themselves" and could not see him. This was a result of the transference of affection phenomenon.

How the Transfer Works

The transfer technique is like an interview, but with one exception: You'll direct the conversation with your man toward events in your man's life that have emotional content. Ask him to describe his inhibitions, anxiety, guilt, hostility, anger, pleasure, competence, self-esteem, lust, sorrow, love, jealousy, and dependency. "Why do you seem anxious?" or "Did you enjoy it?" or a reference to another state of mind will get you started.

Ask questions and listen to his answers. As a listener, have "big ears," allowing the man to say anything that gives him relief, much like a confession. He need not even be completely frank in the beginning; that will come later. As he talks, he will expose to you his true thoughts and his true self. When you begin this transfer process, don't encourage your man into subjects that are unpleasant to him or subjects that he views as particularly private. It won't be long before he naturally tells you all, including the intimacies of his sex life.

You want him to learn the habit of confiding in you. Encourage him to talk to you as if he were talking out loud to himself. Don't be offended at anything he says. Instead, let his mind explore all possibilities. If you are shocked too easily, you may appear unsophisticated or mentally weak.

There are various techniques for getting men to disclose their secrets, problems, or peculiarities. Our method is as simple as asking questions, like "What does this bring to mind?" This "induced monologue" is the principal method for uncovering unconscious motives. Ask your man to utter everything that comes into his mind without exception. The shrewd woman, if she chooses, may then exploit these positive feelings to get loyalty, affection, and passion from her grateful man.

Remember, allow the man to communicate whatever he likes. Wait patiently and quietly until he begins to tell you all. It is advantageous to start with his early childhood or his schooling. His conscience probably was weak in those years. He now should feel freer about telling on himself, so to speak. If, in the meantime, you keep your past out of the conversation and don't compete for an analysis of yourself, you will be extraordinarily successful.

As your man is recalling emotional events of the past, you might initially be bored, but he isn't. He is carrying on as if the events were happening now instead of just being remembered. Give him praise where appropriate, such as when he tells you about his earlier accomplishments. Give him empathy when he tells you his doubts and fears. He will enjoy the pleasure of speaking freely. You are going to have a happy man.

Let your man initiate conversations, then guide their direction. Do not interfere with what he is saying or raise other topics. Avoid expressing your own opinions, ideas, and attitudes. You'll have full power to express yourself, but do it later, after he transfers affection to you and you know he's the one for you. Above all, avoid making important disclosures about yourself; you don't want him to artificially change his responses to get you in the sack. Let him talk until he is finished on every subject he raises while you remain quiet.

ASKING HIM QUESTIONS

When you ask him questions, be sure the questions are predominantly, but not totally, positive. Review the following list of fifty possible questions to see their general positive slant. When your man answers these questions, you will feel the warmth and the inner strength you will gain from his transference.

These are only a few of the questions you can ask, so use your imagination and make up your own. Once your man has warmed up by answering some of these questions, and you don't laugh or scold or compete with him by revealing your own attitudes, he'll probably talk your ears off. Great! Then, to be sure you've exhausted him on a subject, gently prod with "Is there more?"

1. What were you like as a little boy?
2. What is the first event in your youth that you can remember?
3. Who were your favorite relatives?
4. What games, clubs, hobbies, relatives, sports, or other activities did you like or dislike, and why?
5. What parts of your childhood would you like to relive?
6. What do you remember about your first day of school?
7. Did you enjoy school? Why or why not? What was your favorite grade and favorite teacher?
8. What do you remember best about your home life?
9. What do you think is the most important factor in a home life?
10. What do you consider the most important part of growing up?
11. At what age did you first like girls?
12. At what age did you begin puberty?
13. Did you ever want to be a girl?
14. Did you enjoy having brothers? Sisters? Why?
15. Did you have sufficient money and clothes as a youth? Were you content with your looks?
16. How did you see yourself then? And now?
17. Who was your first date? Where did you go?
18. Who were your other dates or steadies? What did you like and dislike about each one?
19. What jobs did you have?
20. What is the extent of your education and job experiences? What were your emotional reactions to your job, your fellow employees, and your bosses? What were your ambitions?
21. What do you think your natural gifts are?

22. What do you consider your strong points? Weak points?
23. What is your medical history? Dental history?
24. What is presently your favorite holiday, music, TV program, and pastime?
25. Have you ever built anything? What was it?
26. If you had a million dollars, what would you do?
27. If you were to cast yourself in a movie, in what role would it be?
28. What is your idea of an ideal woman?
29. Do you like pets?
30. What are your thoughts on dress?
31. If you could be anything you wanted to be, what would you choose?
32. Who are the ten most important people in your life?
33. Do you have any hatreds?
34. Who are your friends?
35. What characteristics in people do you respect? Hate?
36. Where would you like to live? What country, state, city, house, apartment?
37. If you could exchange physical features with others, what would you exchange, and with whom?
38. What are your views on growing old?
39. How religious is your family?
40. What has been the best year of your life so far? Why?
41. Who educated you in sex? What are your sexual experiences?
42. What are your views on sex? Who should teach sex and who should indulge?
43. What are your political views?
44. Where would you like to be buried? Are you against cremation?
45. If you had to be stranded on an island with only one other person (not yourself), who would you choose?
46. What one book would you bring to your island?
47. What are your prejudices?

48. How would you complete the sentence, "Man is
    _____"?
49. Do you believe in an afterlife?
50. Have you ever fathered a child? Do you want children?

Use these questions to get him to open up to you. Let his answers serve as the starting point for other questions you'd like to ask him.

Don't ask these questions all in one sitting, or administer them as a school exam. Do not, under any circumstances, hand him this list as a questionnaire and ask him to fill it out. You may receive his answers, but not the transference of affection. Instead, use the questions to loosen his tongue, and use them only when he runs out of his own ideas. Then start him going again about himself.

Additional Questions

When you prepare questions for your man, go back to his past, to his schooling. Some of these questions depend on his background, or on his answers to prior questions. Here are the sort of follow-up questions you might ask him:

1. What did you enjoy most about your computer?
2. Who was your best boss?
3. What first evoked your interest in engineering?
4. What additional training would you pursue?
5. What are your strongest leadership traits?

Framing Your Questions

Suppose the two of you are watching a television program. You can let the program serve as a backdrop for your questions.

Don't ask: When did you first watch this show?

Unless you ask: *Why* do you like the show?

Don't ask: Who is your favorite character?
Unless you ask: *Why* do you like that person?

Don't ask: What is your favorite sport?
Unless you ask: *Why* do you like it?

You and Your Competition

Do you know all about your man's first love affair, his first car, his first job, and everything else that is important to him? If you don't know these details, you're failing to gain all his affections because you don't have the "open ear" that he needs. Your man is, has been, and will be vulnerable to another woman who knows the transfer of affection technique. If she induces such a monologue from your man, encouraging him to talk about you, he is likely to transfer his affections from you to her.

Since other women can use the transfer of love technique against you, use it regularly to retain your man's love. If your man's affection for you isn't deep enough, transference is a true and tested way to gain and increase his affection.

A number of women think so much of themselves that they honestly believe other women can't use the transference of love technique on their men. They would bet everything that their fellows would not relate the events of their lives to someone else. But these women would lose their bet. All men are small boys at heart. They love to tell their stories!

Stealing Love

If you aren't the first woman your fellow has loved, encourage him to talk about his love interests. Do this whether his loves are past or present. These revelations may injure your pride, but will be effective in enticing him into your corner. A woman often makes the mistake of not asking her fellow about the experiences he's had with other women. Her jealousies won't permit him to talk about them, claiming the man's affairs are too painful for her to discuss. Jealousy stands in the way of this transfer! Your relationship will be in jeopardy without complete open listening and knowledge about him, and you will have missed out on the man's total affection.

The best shortcut to a man's heart is to capture the love that he already feels for another woman. You can gather all the love in the man's heart and have him transfer this affection to you. Every man who has ever loved can be made to love again—to fall in love with you. Examine this idea closely. *A woman with a working knowledge of this technique can transfer to herself the affections that a man holds for another woman.*

GOALS AND STRATEGIES

If you have found open communication with your fellow difficult, he is likely to remain reticent. But keep on trying. Keep on telling him that you want to know about him because he's so unique and interesting. With a little bit of prodding, chances are great that he will start communicating with you. Keep in mind that, as you ask questions of your fellow, your purpose is twofold:

1. You want to hear every incident of his life that had any emotional feelings attached to it so that he will transfer his affection to you.
2. Just as important, you are planning for the future. To become his indispensable mate, you must always be his empathetic listener. Encourage him to talk to you as if he is talking out loud to himself.

Let Him Talk

Let your fellow talk openly, without interrupting him or trying to keep his discourse consistent. Even if his answers are not in a logical sequence, they are in an emotional sequence—one that makes sense to him. If he stops and waits for you to give him some comments about yourself, do so, and repeat some minor incident of your life. Then turn the conversation back to him.

Don't criticize him yet. This comes later, after he transfers his affection to you. He won't speak freely if you ridicule, criticize, or condemn him for exposing his thoughts, feelings, or experiences.

Transference of affection produces profound and lasting changes in the feelings, attitudes, values, and activities of your fellow. Most important, these changes are made in your direction.

Once you've explored all your man's thoughts, especially those attached to emotions, there's no reason why you can't reap the benefits of all your man has shared with you. A reminiscence of your pleasant occasions together enables him to relive these moments and reinforce his emotions toward you.

Usually it takes a man about a hundred hours to reveal all the emotional tales of his life. Let him invest emotions in you during these hundred hours. You'll know you've reached the end of his emotional history when he starts repeating his stories or says, "I've never told this to anyone before."

Create a friendly atmosphere when asking questions and listening to your man. Like the psychologist, make sure he is comfortable and not hungry or thirsty, and feels it's a private conversation. Listening warmly has a strong seductive effect that bonds the speaker to the listener. You'll get his loyalty and love, and his increasing desire to have you. He will enjoy talking to you and being with you every day. He will seek you above all others and want to make this relationship permanent.

Consider the possibility of getting a man to transfer his affections to you even without being in your presence. It can happen—with a telephone or computer. Letters and e-mail can help provide the transfer if you've met him and have personal contact as well.

chapter 7

Enhancing Yourself

Once you select your future husband and help him fall in love with you, you need to enhance your relationship so that it ultimately attains the fullness and completeness both of you expect from marriage.

A relationship does not develop on its own. It takes nurturing, even if the two people are in love. You'll both need to expend considerable effort to bond your two lives together and become one.

Even if a relationship begins with physical attraction and culminates in lovemaking, the intermediate steps require conversation. Don't let any gaps in your communication skills destroy the relationship. Talk your way into his heart.

ENHANCING YOUR SELF-WORTH

You'll do better with men if you increase your own self-worth. These two areas are likely to be of importance to many men:

1. Your background, level of general intelligence, culture, and speech pattern.
2. Your specific knowledge about him—his livelihood and his avocations.

To deal successfully with a man, you need to know something about his job, his career, his business, his sports and hobbies, and other interests that he has. You may have your own job or profession, but you'll need at least conversational familiarity with what he does, whether that's pizza delivery, beer making, engineering, carpentry, or any other field of his. Here are some shortcuts you can use to feel more secure with him.

Mental Stimulation

You can charm your fellow with sweetness and kindness, but those are only temporary enticements for him. Boredom can set in quickly. A better way to build a permanent relationship is to provide him with mental stimulation.

Most men expect their women to be knowledgeable about current events. Read newspapers and magazines to enhance your general knowledge, or rely on other media. Then be sure to watch the news each day on television or the Internet, especially if you haven't read the newspaper. Stimulate your own thinking and gain awareness of the world around you by going to a bookstore or library or using the Internet to learn more about your fellow's occupation, avocation, and current events. Then help him appear knowledgeable with his colleagues by keeping him informed.

You can dazzle your man by providing him with new ideas to think about. He'll develop a hunger, and then a need, for the mental stimulation these new ideas provide.

Learn at least one new thing each week that *he doesn't know!* He might complain about you showing off your learning, but his image of you will change for the better.

Be prepared to talk about some interesting aspect of your work or an outside activity. Your man should be comfortable in knowing what you'll say about yourself when you meet his family and friends. Have at least one twenty-minute speech or anecdote you could deliver if you needed to. Develop your knowledge of one specific "public topic" that could be important to your fellow. I'll discuss public topics later.

Speech Patterns

You always try to look the best that you can. Be all that you can be when it comes to the sounds you make as well. Be conscious of the words you choose For example, instead of using the word *smell* as a noun, use *odor, aroma, scent,* or *fragrance* to describe what you mean. Don't use big fancy words when plain ordinary words will do, or you'll sound pompous, pretentious, and phony. Don't let poor diction or weak vocabulary impede your relationship. If your speech is deficient, your fellow might view you as a member of a lower social class than he is and reject you for marriage.

Enhance your man's image of you by recalling words you know but have been too lazy to use. If possible, correct his speech by paraphrasing what he says in a superior vocabulary. For example, if he says, "I'm mad," you say, "You mean you're angry—dogs go mad." Every time you improve his conversation, you will increase his respect for your mind. But remember to never correct him in public.

Your rate of speech can categorize you as either a thinker or a scatterbrain. A deliberate delivery of words conveys intelligence, while overly rapid speech indicates impulsiveness and can make your words sound insignificant. Avoid incomplete sentences. Think before you speak. If you believe you're not taken as seriously as you'd like, slow your rate of speech. Form complete sentences in your mind before speaking. Your speech will improve if you talk to a man as if your teachers were eavesdropping. Then watch for the results. A man who listens to you will recognize your careful speech, and believe that you were careful in selecting him.

Show Enthusiasm

Show enthusiasm over *something*. Enthusiasm is contagious. Even if your listener doesn't know much about what delights you, your enthusiasm will incite his. He'll feel alive and vibrant being with you. No man wants the responsibility of entertaining a woman forever. He wants to know that she has her own interests in life. He expects her to do her part in keeping herself happy and keeping him amused.

Use Your Mind to Attract Men

Show your intellectual curiosity whenever possible. Start by asking the man questions about his own field of knowledge so that he will answer with ease. Then ask harder questions. His respect for your intelligence will be raised in proportion to the number of intelligent questions you ask. You will start to acquire the "meeting of the minds" necessary for a successful marriage.

It is of crucial importance that the man believes that you have the mental capacity to think clearly and deeply. If he believes that you can think as well as he thinks, then he will believe you can feel as deeply as he does. He's looking for a woman whom he thinks is worthy of him and raising his children, a woman who has the mental capacity to understand his ideas, his feelings, and his passions. He'll accept compliments and praise from any source, but he will eventually make you earn his mental respect. If he doesn't respect your mind, he won't marry you.

His Job or Career

No man will ever intimidate you mentally if you know about his field. Learn about the specific purposes and limitations of his profession or trade. You can then speak knowledgeably and impress him with your interest. It is especially important to learn the gaps in his knowledge so that if he tries to overwhelm you with the importance of his job, you can diminish it to its appropriate level.

Rarely will a person marry someone who puts him up on a pedestal. Don't be overly impressed by a man's job, no matter what it is. Never allow any man to treat you as inferior just because you lack the knowledge to perform his job. The mere knowledge of a specialized trade or profession does not add materially to a man's wisdom. Each man overemphasizes the importance of his specialty or trade to gain identity and recognition. He wants you to believe that his occupation requires a lifetime of constant practice, but this usually is far from the case.

Each occupation has a vocabulary all its own. If you learn a few dozen words he uses in his job, you'll be very impressive to him. He will be pleased by your interest. Read a how-to book that pertains to his occupation. For example:

➤ If your man is a carpenter, be able to identify the different types of saws he uses. Later, learn about his drill bits, woods, fasteners, and designs.

➤ If your man is an attorney, be able to identify the law books he uses. Later, learn about the courts in which he practices, the type of clients he represents, and the judges he appears before.

➤ If your fellow makes pizza, be able to identify the pizza-making steps. Later, learn how he prepares the dough, the refrigeration process, kneading, and baking times.

➤ If your fellow is a government worker, be able to identify the specific area in which he works. Later, learn the specifics of what he does for the government, his rank or grade, the people who are above him or below, and the paperwork that the job entails.

➤ If your fellow is a dentist, be able to identify his dentistry tools. Later, learn the names of the teeth and common dental procedures.

➢ If your fellow is a student, be able to identify his course of study. Later, learn the basics of his subject and ask to read his papers and presentations.

➢ If your fellow is a factory worker, be able to identify what he does in the factory. Later, learn the names of the manufacturing equipment and how his activity fits into the entire operation of the factory.

➢ If your fellow is a mortician, learn what caskets he sells. Later, learn about his embalming methods and his skills in dealing with the bereaved.

➢ If your fellow is unemployed, learn about the opportunities he's seeking. Later, when he does get a job, learn about that job.

➢ If your fellow is a musician, learn about his instrument. Later, learn about his role in his musical group and the music he performs, and hear what he's recorded or written.

You should be pleased to gain more information about your fellow's job and career. Later in this book, I'll show you how to bond with him based on the information you're receiving now. If you don't really seek that information about your fellow and his career, you might not want him for a long-term relationship.

That Awe-some Feeling

Don't remain in awe of your fellow's career. If you want to marry a doctor, for example, you need to know something about the field of medicine, especially its limitations, so that you aren't in awe of him.

To appreciate how little is known in medicine, examine a medical dictionary. You will find many terms ending in *-itis*, which indicates "condition," and *-osis*, which means "condition of." These terms are often used when the illness remains a mystery to the field of medicine. *Dermatitis* is just a fancy word for a skin condition, *arthritis* is a swelling of a joint, *sinusitis* is a sinus inflammation, and *halitosis* is just another word for bad breath. Don't be afraid to focus on what your fellow doesn't know.

By learning a few Latin and Greek roots and suffixes, you will more readily understand medical vocabulary. Thus, *-tomy* means "to cut out," and *mastos* means "breast," so a mastectomy is the surgical removal of a breast. *Hyster* is Greek for "uterus," so hysterectomy is the removal of the uterus.

Once you master the mystery of medical terms, you'll be better prepared to date a physician and speak intelligently with him. Use your knowledge to ask about the causes of various diseases ending in *-itis* and various conditions ending in *-osis*. A doctor may use jargon to sound more impressive. What would you think of a physician who tells you, "You have a swollen breast and I can't explain exactly why. You may have scratched your nipple or something may be wrong inside." You would be impressed only if he used the medical terms: "You are suffering from mastitis. In my opinion it could be caused by an abrasion of the areola or a bacterial infection."

If you are interested in a physician, you need to speak his language; your general familiarity with medical terms will help make you more desirable to him. Follow the same process with any professional.

His Business

Your fellow might be fortunate enough to have a business of his own. You'll be better able to bond with him if you discuss his business. Do you know these basics?

➤ What does his business actually do?
➤ With whom is he in business?
➤ What type of customers does he have?
➤ Who are his suppliers?
➤ Where are his business locations?
➤ Who are his competitors?

➤ Who does he fear the most?
➤ Who are his best business friends?
➤ How does he promote his business?
➤ Who works for him?

His Sports

You and your fellow will be better able to bond if you can converse with him about his favorite sport, whether he's a player or a fan. This bonding works even if you and your fellow like different sports.

➤ How is the sport played?
➤ What position does he play?
➤ Where do the games take place?
➤ What teams are in the league?
➤ Who are the players on his team?
➤ Who are the players he admires?
➤ Who are the players he fears?
➤ Who finances the team?
➤ What are the team's slogans and motto?
➤ What is the team's standing in the league?

If a sport is important to your fellow, and you don't have much knowledge about it or desire to learn about it, he may not be your ideal mate.

His Hobbies

You and your fellow might have different hobbies, but you should be able to converse with him about the specifics of his hobby. If your fellow's hobby is important to him, and you're unwilling to know the specifics, he very well might not be your ideal mate.

SPEAKING OF YOU

Now it's time to talk about you. Aren't you glad you didn't tell all those strange men you met the intimate details of your life? You remember them, the 90 or 95 percent of the men you met with those early hellos and have since eliminated from further consideration? Now you have reached the stage where you enjoy the men you are with and consider each as a potential mate. As you make the transition between casual dating and a serious relationship, you need to know what to say to these few select men who deserve to hear about *you*.

The Importance of Communication

Once a relationship becomes serious, you both need to speak up and express your thoughts and feelings. If either of you is overly private or withdrawn, the relationship will be in jeopardy. If the man is too quiet, do not assume all is well. Draw him out. Even if you are shy or reserved, you need to tell him about yourself.

Some quiet people take great pride in being self-sufficient, even to the point of hiding their personal needs or wants. These folks display affection by performing their duties in their relationship, but not by talking about the relationship or its problems. Expressive people take pride in verbalizing their wants and needs. Their goal is total communication, and they show affection by talking about whatever is on their minds.

Some people have a very strong sense of personal privacy and consider inquisitive people to be nosy. Yet people who are caring and concerned will inquire about a loved one's private life and expect some answers. When these responses are not forthcoming, the silence is interpreted as a lack of love, trust, or interest in maintaining a relationship.

If you are the emotionally quiet type, an expressive person may view you as withdrawn, arrogant, unfriendly, or cold. If you're expressive, a silent type may view you as aggressive, rude, or over-bearing. These differences are a source of misunderstanding. In the following examples, she is taciturn and he is expressive, but in some relationships it's the man who's quiet.

SHE: He should know that I love him and that I'm unhappy with the rut we are in.

HE: She must be pleased with our relationship or she would speak up.

SHE: He is supposed to know what I'm thinking. He should know my needs and I shouldn't have to ask him for what I want. If I'm thirsty, he should bring me a drink without expecting me to ask.

HE: I'm dying of thirst. What good stuff do you have in the refrigerator?

SHE: I'll bite my lip for now. If I can't stand the overall relationship, there's no point in complaining. I'll get out.

HE: If something is bothering me, you're going to hear about it. I can't read your mind, so how can I expect you to read mine?

Taciturn and expressive people are likely to misinterpret each other's intentions. To avoid this sort of misunderstanding, encourage your partner to spend at least fifteen minutes each day telling you what's on his mind, and be sure to express yourself as well.

WHAT SHOULD YOU TALK ABOUT?

The subject matter of your discussions can be divided into three categories:

1. Public topics
2. Private topics
3. Mutual topics

Whenever you discuss a topic, consider whether the topic is public, private, or mutual. Surprisingly, you should discuss public topics and mutual topics, but avoid private subjects! People who talk about private topics are often boring. Private topics are those with which you alone—not your fellow—are familiar.

Public Topics

A topic is "public" if strangers are aware of the topic and could plausibly participate in the discussion. Public topics, in contrast to private topics, are good topics for discussion. Both of you are likely to be familiar with the subject matter. Years ago, many women were taught to avoid controversial topics such as sex, religion, and politics. Turn this on its head in a dating context. *Don't* avoid controversial topics; it's part of the mate-selection process. Events described in the media are good examples of discussion topics. Here are some public topics:

> ➤ The weather
> ➤ An athletic championship
> ➤ Politics
> ➤ Abortion
> ➤ A new clothing style
> ➤ An upcoming election
> ➤ Political unrest in a foreign country
> ➤ A murder or kidnapping
> ➤ Rumors of a new cure for cancer
> ➤ A current film or concert

Private Topics

Topics are "private" when they pertain to the individual lives of you or your man, but not to both. Here are some examples:

> ➤ When you first meet a man and he doesn't know your family, discussions about your relatives are private.

➤ Unless your man works with you or knows your co-workers, discussions about your job and your co-workers are private.

➤ Unless your fellow is a neighbor, conversations about your neighborhood are private.

➤ Discussions about vacations you took before you met him are private unless he has also been to these vacation spots.

➤ Discussions about your friends are private unless he knows them, too.

You may see events vividly in your mind, but it's often difficult to describe these situations to your fellow or evoke his interest. Describe these events only when the man is familiar with the people, places, or events. Then let him know about these events in a way that evokes his interest and curiosity.

Mutual Topics

Mutual topics pertain both to you and your man. They're fully appropriate on a date. These are some examples:

➤ Foods that you both enjoy.

➤ Plans for your next date.

➤ The effect that a public event has on the two of you.

➤ Impressions of each other when you first met.

➤ How your career goals interrelate with his.

ACCENTUATE THE POSITIVE

Present yourself in the best possible light. There are times when you need to brag, to make self-serving statements such as "I was the smartest student in math class" or "I've been told many times that I have lovely hair." If you want the man to believe that you are beautiful and intelligent, you have to show him that you believe in yourself by stating it.

Place pleasant thoughts about yourself into conversations

whenever you can. If he compliments you, thank him, but reinforce the compliment by repeating the statement. If he says that you're pretty, for instance, say, "I'm glad you think I'm pretty." As soon as one positive idea about you reaches him, create another. Bombard him with positive thoughts. Let him *know* that you're a treasure!

Make sure that your claim is sound and that your assertions are reasonable. If you claim that you are Princess Jasmine, the daughter of the House of Solomon, no man will believe you. Don't exaggerate your statements or resort to lying. Not only are false statements worthless, but the man will hold them against you as well.

What About Your Weaknesses?

Do you have a birthmark or a more serious physical flaw? If so, some of the men you have dated may have avoided discussing the flaw in order to spare your feelings. If they did mention the flaw, you might have asked them not to mention it again. But whether your weakness is a wart on your nose, a limp, or fifty extra pounds, it will not go away because it is unmentioned. Instead, pretending the defect does not exist isolates the two of you from each other.

Do mention your obvious defects, but don't do it in a way designed to elicit sympathy. It's better to say, "Did you ever see such a scar?" than to pretend that the scar doesn't exist. But wait until you and he are interested in each other before you bring up this defect. If you don't appear overly concerned about your imperfections, he'll likely ignore them, too.

Some women accentuate the negative about themselves, hoping the fellow will counteract the negative statement. She'll state that she's flat-chested, short, and has a big nose, for instance, hoping that her fellow will reply, "I love short flat-chested women with big noses." She is skipping steps in the bonding process, because she has no way of knowing whether this is a statement he would make or whether it would be truthful. All too often, though, the woman who exaggerates her negative attributes is conditioning her fellow to view them as important.

Don't dwell on your defects. Your fellow can see the physical imperfections, whether it's big ears, poor skin, unruly hair, or crooked teeth. If you feel strongly about your defects and must purge yourself with a confession, confess to your parents or relatives, or to friends whom you aren't planning to wed.

Avoiding a Negative Image

A man needs a relationship with a woman with whom he can forget his own mental conflicts. He's looking for a friend and a companion in sex, not someone who insists on frequently reciting her personal medical history, her fears about money, and her physical and mental deficiencies. If you load the man down with undesirable images about yourself, it will ultimately lead to your rejection.

If you went out to buy an automobile and the salesman kept reminding you that the car could get flat tires, that the radiator might leak, that the transmission could break down, and that the upholstery will probably fade, you would find another salesman, even if you liked the car!

Some women boast about their poor health, poor vision, allergies, lack of stamina, or broken-down arches as if these deficiencies were attributes. Even if a man admires daintiness (and many do not), he will not view frailty as a virtue.

In addition, the man may intensify any statements you make against yourself. If a woman says "I am an unworthy soul, a wretched person, ignorant, ugly, decrepit," and so on, the man is likely to believe her even if these things aren't true. Present yourself honestly, but emphasize the positive.

Eventually, if the relationship becomes serious and progresses toward marriage, you and your man should discuss such topics as your sexual needs, your financial liabilities, and the relatives for whom you are responsible. But wait for the relationship to develop before having these discussions, and don't dwell on your own weaknesses along the way.

WATCH WHAT YOU SAY

Here are eight subject areas that require special handling in the developing stages of a relationship:

1. *Religion and ethnic group.* Don't attempt to convert your fellow to your religion; nor should you be chauvinistic about your ethnic group. If either has anything to offer, your example will convey it.

2. *Survival.* Unless the facts are otherwise, let him know that you're capable of supporting yourself. If you're really in economic stress, show him that you can "grin and bear it," and that you're optimistic about the future.

3. *Talking dirty.* Sometimes a woman will use dirty words when she is with a man in an attempt to appear down-to-earth. The result, however, may be quite the contrary, especially if the man is older and more traditional. Such a man will visualize the word, and the woman will be degraded in his mind. Know your audience, and avoid these consequences! Wait until he uses these words first.

4. *Sounding childish.* Many women are passed by for marriage because they don't speak like mature adults. Even though they wouldn't consider dressing for a date in diapers, or arranging their hair in pigtails, their discussions with a man may be loaded with immature nonsense and girlish giggles. Please, if you're old enough to read this material, don't giggle!

5. *Pseudo-sciences.* When did you last see a horoscope in a men's magazine? Very few men believe in astrology, fortune-

telling, or reincarnation. If you believe in such things, realize that most men are likely to hold these beliefs against you.

6. *Irrational fears.* Displays of fear that are not founded on good reason are harmful to your relationship with men. We're all familiar with the cartoon of a woman perched on a chair because a tiny mouse is scurrying across her kitchen floor. Don't shriek at the sight of a bug or a mouse; your man will lose respect for you. A man will view you very negatively if you act squeamish at the sight of blood. He'll think you're incapable of taking care of him if he becomes sick or injured. Once he reaches this conclusion, he is likely to pass you by as a potential mate. Irrational fears may be held against you, whether it's a fear of moving out of your neighborhood or a fear of elevators.

7. *Sounding like a parasite.* Some women act like parasites. They tell their friends, only partially in jest, that it would be great to have a rich old man with one foot in the grave and the other on a banana peel. This idea is repulsive to men. If you're not a parasite, don't sound like one. A woman who is not parasitical may inadvertently give such an impression by talking about how she dislikes work, enjoys elaborate vacations, longs to travel, and loves clothing and jewelry. She may brag that she's unable to cook or entertain herself. Then she wonders why men pass her by for marriage. Don't let such careless statements keep you from marriage. Think about what you say, and avoid statements that may make you sound parasitical.

8. *Sounding like a prostitute.* Some women demand expensive gifts because they are unwilling to "sell themselves cheaply." They are afraid to give something away, namely themselves, without sufficient payment. But if you expect the man to pay for the pleasure of your company, he is likely to see you as a prostitute rather than a future wife.

Don't ask for gifts or for the man to spend money on you. Don't even hint. If he offers you an expensive gift, accept it only if you tell him he can have it back. A man who finds a truly considerate woman will eventually be generous, but no man wants to believe that he must spend great sums to enjoy good female companionship.

chapter 8

Praising and Criticizing the One You Love

Some women believe they can capture a man's heart by enticing him with their beauty, or cooking, or lovemaking. Others are sure they can garner a man's affections by demonstrating their own ingenuity, abilities, or achievements. But there is a far better strategy: Act like his wife and treat him like your husband. How do you do this? By praising and criticizing him as a wife would. The key to a man's heart is balancing your praise with criticism while recognizing that he's unique.

Praise and criticism generate the intense emotions that enable a relationship to develop. Equally important, praise and criticism are expected as part of everyday family life, particularly in relationships between husband and wife. Everyone wants praise, but because of your upbringing, you associate a certain level of criticism with love.

The man's parents made him feel special, loved, and in a class by himself. They referred to him as "our precious child," yet they were always pointing out his imperfections. This is a pattern of behavior you can follow and use to your advantage.

THE MAN'S STRIVING FOR UNIQUENESS

A man is a strange creature, for he wants two opposite things. A normal man does not enjoy being a hermit, but needs to be accepted into a group. He will even conform his behavior to join this group. Yet once he's accepted by the group, he then feels the need to stand out from it. In other words, if your man is not a member of a club, he will fight to join. But once he's a member of this club, he's satisfied only if he's its leader.

A man, by his nature, cannot be happy without feeling that he's unique. Listen to men's conversations the next time you attend a gathering. Each man tells stories that show his success. He describes his cleverness, how smart he is, how he outwitted someone else.

Be a clever woman and tell your man, "You are unique," "You are so different from other men," "There's something special about you." You'll gain his love as you reinforce the concept that he is special. He will become addicted to your praise, especially when you mix it with criticism, because he will recognize that your praise is genuine.

Ask your man, "When did you first realize that you were unique?" You may be amazed at his answer. He may have felt "different" since he was four or five! The more intelligent the man, the earlier he felt unique. He may even remember the specific circumstances when he realized his uniqueness.

A woman can take advantage of a man's need to be unique to lead him into a strong relationship with her. The woman, by listening and adding her approval to what she hears, controls the amount of uniqueness she permits her man to believe about himself. If the man believes that you have recognized his uniqueness, he will be seeking you out above all others!

Much as your mother told you that, one day, someone would come into your life and recognize just how special and unique you really are, his mother told this to him, too. He is expecting someone to come into his life and recognize how special and unique he is. He's casually dating now, in anticipation that somewhere, somehow, someone will appear. You can fulfill his mother's prophecy, and be the woman who's just right for him. You do this if you find him unique and special and let him know it.

Discovering His Uniqueness

Discover your man's feeling of uniqueness. Encourage him to tell you how different he is from other men. Here are examples of what you could be asking him to tell you about:

➤ His superiority in his job
➤ His witty conversation with his boss
➤ Praise he receives from others in his occupation
➤ Honors he received in school
➤ How dumb or unsophisticated people around him are
➤ His unusual experiences
➤ The people he's impressed
➤ His proudest moments
➤ The women who've wanted him
➤ His greatest athletic accomplishment

Reinforce the characteristics of your fellow's personality that demonstrate his uniqueness. Smile or nod with approval over any story that shows his superiority over the next guy. The easiest ways to please him are to listen, add your approval to what you hear, and tell him how unique he is.

One of my clients stepped into an elevator and saw a man whom she was attracted to. The building was small, there were few floors, and the elevator was fast. She had less than thirty seconds to act. She looked at this fellow and said, "I don't know you, but I sure wish I did. There's something unique about you!" She left the elevator without giving him her name. The man was stunned. He combed the building looking for her, and they're now married.

What Men Do to Be Unique

A man's need to be unique may cause him to undertake unusual activities. Here are some "unique" activities. Which of these apply to your man?

➤ Indulging in dangerous sports
➤ Having an exotic pet
➤ Piercing a body part in an unusual place
➤ Having an unusual mustache
➤ Telling outrageous stories or exaggerating them
➤ Wearing garish clothing or expensive jewelry
➤ Overspending or tipping outrageous amounts
➤ Being a daredevil
➤ Driving an unusual automobile
➤ Engaging in activities that he thinks are beyond what the ordinary man would do

After you are comfortable with your man, and he deluges you with stories of his achievements, encourage him to talk even more. The longer he talks, the more firmly entrenched he becomes with you. Your man will sell himself to exhaustion if you allow it. When he reaches exhaustion, assure him how important he is by repeating his best pitches as if you had thought of them yourself.

Broadcasting His Uniqueness

Always praise your man in front of his immediate family, co-workers, and friends. Be his advocate and speak well of him to these individuals. Make comments such as "If anyone can do it, he can!" Remove that praise privately if it inflates his ego. A comment such as "Your boss really believed everything I said about you" will suffice.

Here are some more positive statements you can make on his behalf:

➤ He's in a class by himself.
➤ My boyfriend is the most unusual man I know.
➤ He's the best.
➤ God made him and threw away the mold.

A man needs to feel special in order to be happy, and he looks to a woman to tell him that he is special. His male friends don't reinforce those feelings because they are too preoccupied with their own sense of uniqueness.

Using Superlatives

Use superlatives to help your man feel unique. Tell him he's "the most." Try the following, if you believe they're true:

➤ Most intelligent
➤ Best dressed
➤ Most precious
➤ Sexiest
➤ Most unusual
➤ Most interesting
➤ Most amusing
➤ Most fun
➤ Most ambitious
➤ Most dedicated

Repeat to him and to the world why your man is different from all other men. His ego is such that he will think you're brilliant to recognize his uniqueness! Soon he'll believe his uniqueness because he needs to do so for his own survival and self-image. A man's greatest weakness is his desire to be great. He puts his ego out for public scrutiny to achieve this greatness.

Women compliment each other. They fill their need for approval from their female friends. Men, in contrast, typically won't compliment each other in a social setting. Consider this phrase: *I love your outfit.* A woman might make this statement to a man or a woman, but a man would make this statement only to a woman. Men joust with each other verbally. A fellow might say to a colleague, "I hope you didn't pay more than half price for that shirt." Men have to go elsewhere for approval—to women who recognize their uniqueness.

PRAISING YOUR MAN

Praising your man is essential to your relationship because most men require more praise than criticism. Praise him first, to make sure he is emotionally strong enough to withstand the criticism you'll be handing out later. Don't lie, however. If you don't really find him unique, you should have eliminated him previously from further consideration as a prospective mate. It's not too late. If you can't praise him without lying, don't praise him at all. Say good-bye instead.

Providing and Removing Approval

What do I mean by providing and removing approval? You give approval to someone whenever you praise or compliment that person. You remove approval from someone whenever you criticize them.

The clever woman approves of her fellow, reinforcing his concept of his being special. Her approval costs nothing because words are free. Men become addicted to her words.

Why Men Seek Praise and Approval

A man's mind is in conflict because he believes he is unique, important, desirable, worthy, attractive, and successful. But he must face reality: He's just another worker, not a leader, and he's nothing special mentally or physically. He knows that any athletic achievement, business success, or fame he is enjoying can soon end. His grandiose beliefs make him feel he's a miserable fraud. Let's examine the power of the mind and how nasty it is.

Negative statements are more intense than positive ones. You probably receive more praise than criticism, but you remember the criticism more vividly. So does a man. If I walked up to you and said, "My, you are attractive," you would smile and soon forget my compliment. But if I said, "You have a big nose," you wouldn't soon forget it.

Your mind can be harsh, too. Imagine your response if I were to put a microphone in your hands and ask you to speak. Your mind might cut off your memory bank, and you may not be able to think of anything worthwhile to say! Recall your school days when you knew the answer to an exam question, but your mind went blank at the critical moment when you were called upon to recite.

If your man is receiving honors and basking in their glory, his mind will release some unpleasant memory to deflate his facade. Most men, even under the most ideal conditions, face a hostile world. Since each man needs to feel unique to combat his negative thoughts, he attempts to diminish the next person's importance. A man wants a woman who helps him combat his negative thoughts. You'll attract men if you give praise effectively. Each will develop feelings of gratitude and affection for you.

Trumping the Survival Instinct

Survival is usually the strongest instinct, but a man's pride can sometimes be stronger than his will to live! Vanity is a strong instinct, too. It's almost impossible for a man to release himself from the vanity of being important and accepted. If a man's pride is seriously injured, he'll feel worthless. He'll lose face, and view his life as being insignificant.

A man strives for praise and approval, even to the detriment of his life, health, business, and general well-being. His great pride can interfere with good sense. A newly wealthy man I met paid his chauffeur three times what a well-paid chauffeur ordinarily earned. Why? Because the now-wealthy man had once been the chauffeur to his chauffeur! Just for the sake of having an ex-master as a servant, this man was willing to pay an outrageous price. He was willing to pay for bragging privileges.

Don't let the significance of these incidents pass you by! If your man requires much approval and a large sense of uniqueness to enjoy great happiness, provide them! The greater amount of praise and recognition you can provide, the greater a man's need to keep you near him.

Stinking Thinking

A man seeks diversions as a relief from his "stinking thinking." Men get away from it all so that they can lose themselves by seeing new places, people, and things. Men fish, watch television, work, go to a movie, or do anything that takes their minds off themselves. It is a terrible punishment for a man to be forced to be by himself and reflect upon his past actions. The most hardened criminal cringes at the thought of solitary confinement.

Sexual lovemaking gets the man away from thinking about the problems he faces in life. His mind does not remind him of his failures, bills, anxieties, or any other unpleasantries. But this mental harmony lasts only for a short while; his negative thoughts reappear after he is satisfied.

HOW TO MAKE HIM FEEL IMPORTANT

Now, for those of you who have difficulty imagining how to begin giving praise effectively, start with making your man feel important. Here are two examples. Jane had been happily married for more than thirty years and her children had grown and moved away, leaving her husband as her sole companion. They were strangers when it came to companionship, and hadn't really communicated for years other than about family matters. She knew she had to break through this wall of silence by praising him and recognizing his uniqueness. She paled at the thought of how difficult this would be, and asked me how she could start over.

At that point, before I could respond, a neighborhood youngster, about six years old, dashed into the room to say hello. The boy gave Jane his daily kiss and hug. The boy was extremely fond of her, for she was kind and generous to children. Jane's eyes sparkled when she saw this boy. There was enthusiasm and interest in her voice when she spoke to him about his day. She listened to his account of how he spent his time. She hugged him, tousled his hair, offered him the seat next to her, and gave him milk and cookies. Most important of all, she offered him time to talk about what he wanted to talk about, and she listened with great interest.

My client was making the boy feel important and special. Most women have no trouble giving approval to a six-year-old boy. Your man, six foot one and thirty-six years old, is still a six-year-old when it comes to seeking approval. I told Jane to use this same approach with her husband!

Andrea was a busy middle-management boss with a limited social life. She was frightened by the thought of talking to her dates, although she felt comfortable with people up and down the corporate ladder. While Andrea was thinking about how difficult it was for her to communicate with men on a dating level, Jim, one of her key staff members, walked into her office for his weekly chat.

Andrea sat Jim down and made sure he was reasonably comfortable. She offered him refreshments and the opportunity to discuss anything that was on his mind concerning the business. She listened to him intensely, made mental notes about his positive contributions, and then reiterated his success stories with enthusiasm and interest in her voice. Andrea made her staff member feel important. Once she transferred her talent for listening and praising to her social life, she became highly desirable.

Caressing with Words

Always greet your man by name and with a warm hello. Let him know with your smile that you're happy to see him. Mention his name about once every two to ten minutes when you're chatting.

The sound of his name may be his favorite sound, so use his name frequently.

Your emotional life with a man depends on your tongue. Keep your man happy by caressing him with words. Start with his physical attributes. Tell him that he is handsome; that his glances excite you; that his eyes sparkle. If he has any features that are outstanding, give those features great emphasis. If his looks are different, tell him that although he may not meet the concept of "attractive" for some women, he certainly is handsome enough for you. If you can't do this honestly, find someone else.

Next, praise his thinking. Validate his thoughts by telling him he is intelligent. Even if you disagree with his conclusions and say so, acknowledge that he uses good logic. Of course, it is possible to oversweeten what you tell your man. Still, there are remedies for oversweetening, but rarely are there remedial measures for sourness.

Reflecting the Man to Himself

Your man needs to know what you think of him. Your statements carry impact. Your man cannot see himself and cannot evaluate himself with certainty. He depends on feedback from his female companions to judge himself. A man cannot approach another male as a woman approaches another woman. He can't get the same type of praise from his male friends.

Below are statements you're *not* going to hear among men in normal male conversations:

➤ Don't you think I'm handsome?
➤ Don't I look cute?
➤ Am I sexually desirable?
➤ Is my butt fat?
➤ Which is best for me, mauve or puce?

You can set yourself up as a mirror, reflecting for your man how he appears to the world. He might be taken aback or amused at first, but he will be an ardent listener and will want to hear more. Your ease in showing him to himself will let him know that you are self-assured enough to evaluate him. He will believe what you say since he has no means of contradicting you except by using the opinion of others.

CRITICIZING YOUR MAN

You praised your man to make him feel special. Your recognition of his uniqueness should be the reason you want to provide him with your companionship, with sex, with everything you have to offer. But you must also criticize the one you love, or you will ultimately lose out. Criticism intensifies the relationship because it stirs the man's emotions and brings him to reality. When you balance criticism with praise, the net effect is stronger positive emotions felt toward you.

Criticism is a natural and essential part of any interpersonal relationship. Your parents loved you, but they criticized you. They said, "Your room is a mess" or "You can't come to the dinner table until you comb your hair," or "If you're so smart, why did you get only a B in history?" You associate a certain level of criticism with love, as does your fellow. Criticize your man when you need to do so, but do it with love and acceptance the way your parents did.

You might have praised your fellow too much. You might have increased his feelings of importance, so that he now has delusions of personal grandeur that shut you out and diminish your worth. If so, you can increase your importance by criticizing him. Never let him think he is too good for you.

You'll be most successful in leading the man of your choice into a permanent relationship with you if you show him that you are terrific and wonderful, and that he is extremely fortunate to have you. You do this by showing him your superior qualities and his inadequacies. You may want him because of his superiorities, but you will succeed with him because of his inadequacies. Like most women, despite your faults, you have attributes in which you are superior compared with other women. Your fellow, despite his many good qualities, has attributes in which he is inadequate compared with other men. Your criticism keeps him on his toes!

Stirring His Emotions

When polite conversation becomes boring, then it's time to stir his emotions. Surely you've figured out what areas he may feel sensitive about. Bring up one of those areas and let him know that your fondness or respect for him is not diminished by it. Say to him, "Ben, you're a little short but very darling. I imagine you sometimes wished you were taller." He may welcome the invitation to express some of his frustrations over his height or pride in overcoming feelings of inadequacy about it.

When you tactfully criticize the man you love, he will be pleased with your attention. He should recognize that your criticism is not rejection. You can, and should, criticize him, but always do so with acceptance of him. He will enjoy knowing that you recognize that he is a mere earthling and that you love him anyway.

Early in your relationship, you and your date are both likely to be on your best behavior. Yet over the long run you both will be uncomfortable if you must remain on your best behavior all the time. You need to relax and become comfortable with each other. A certain level of criticism can ease the transition from formal behavior to relaxed informality. Use criticism to nudge him off his pedestal. He does not enjoy pretending to be perfect any more than you do.

Criticize Him in Private

One grave error a woman can make is to criticize her man in front of others. Men hate to be wrong in public, no matter the circumstances. When a woman purchases something from a store and later decides that she doesn't want the item, she does not hesitate to return it. Men, however, rarely return any item they've bought unless it's defective. If men hate to be wrong in public when the situation is trivial, imagine how they detest it when the situation is important.

You can criticize him; just delay it until the two of you are alone.

Distinguishing Criticisms from Insults

Criticize the man, but do not insult him or physically abuse him. There is a big difference between criticism and insults, and this distinction is crucial when you love someone.

Criticisms point out faults, while insults are rude remarks whose purpose is only to incite anger. When you are insulted, you respond to the vehemence of the speaker, not the substance of the statement. When you are criticized, you focus on the substance of what is said. If a statement is both an insult and a criticism, you respond to both what was said *and* the vehemence with which it was said.

Suppose you are in the supermarket checkout line. Another woman accuses you of trying to sneak ahead of her. She calls you a fat, pushy, overbearing, loudmouth slob. These statements are insults, attempts to belittle and anger you.

Suppose, however, that the woman tells you you're sneaking ahead to avoid having people see you in your tattered dress, or that you cut in front of her because you are too nearsighted to see what you're doing. These statements may be insults, but if your dress *is* old or you *are* nearsighted, they're also criticisms because they point out actual faults. Even if you don't feel a sting at the moment you are criticized, these thoughts remain in your mind, and you may feel the sting of criticism in time.

Use noninsulting statements with your fellow. Here are some possible examples:

➤ Your fingernails are filthy.

➤ Fix your collar before you go to work.

➤ You overpaid for your new car.

➤ It's time for a haircut.

➤ You're wearing the wrong shoes.

➤ It's a good thing you think better than you spell.

➤ That tie doesn't match—put on the blue one.

These criticisms will not cause a normal man to flee from you. Criticism has an important role in your relationship with men, but insults do not.

A MAN'S FEELING OF INADEQUACY

Every person suffers from feelings of inadequacy, but men usually suffer more than women. Men compare themselves in a sharply unfavorable manner with other men. Women are less harsh when they compare themselves with other women. A woman may think, *Well, she's richer, but I'm younger.* The woman is kinder to herself in self-judgments.

Society encourages men to compete. Men take jabs at each other rather than being supportive. A bald man may be affectionately referred to by his male friends as "Melonhead." Women friends don't tease one another in this way. Imagine women friends calling each other "Moose" or "Thunderthighs"!

Every man—and every woman—suffers from feelings of being inadequate. When you understand these men's feelings of inadequacy, you should have greater self-confidence in dealing with them. Isn't a man easier to approach if you realize that no matter how desirable he appears to you, he is suffering more from his feelings of being inadequate than you are?

Many men will talk freely about their feelings of being inadequate with someone who approaches the subject empathetically and appears intelligent. As he talks about his weaknesses and failures, he will become more comfortable with you than others.

You will become very knowledgeable about him. Discover these inadequacies early in the relationship. Keep them in mind and consider his faults and his attributes in determining whether he is the right man for you.

USING HIS FEELINGS OF INADEQUACY

The key to successful criticism of a man is to understand his specific feelings of being inadequate. This knowledge can empower you as you develop a continuing relationship with him.

His Facade

Every man, like every woman, has feelings of being superior and of being inadequate. You can easily learn about your fellow's feelings of being superior, but it's harder for you to uncover his feelings of inadequacy. The crucial step in discovering these feelings is to pierce through the image or facade he presents to the world. But what is a facade?

The elaborate and decorative front of a building is called a facade. Every man has a face or facade that he holds out to the public, like a suit of armor. When you meet a man, you see him initially as if he's wearing his suit of armor. He is hiding his innermost thoughts and conflicts, his passions and desires. You can reach him by removing his facade, exposing his feelings of being inadequate. Here's how to get that information:

➤ Start with the general inadequacies that men suffer.
➤ Ask him about himself.
➤ Be alert to admissions he makes.
➤ Watch his demeanor with others.

Get this information only in private. Then watch carefully for his reactions. His feelings of inadequacies are the basic keys to his behavior with you.

Limits on Your Criticism of Him

Use your man's most common and most devastating feelings of inadequacy when you need to criticize him. The goal is to make your man dependent on your acceptance and your approval. Criticize him to keep control of your relationship. When you criticize the man, attack him on any of his feelings of inadequacies as you wish, but follow these limitations:

➤ Do not remove from him his feeling that he is unique.
➤ Do not challenge his zeniths.
➤ Do not attack his sexuality.
➤ Do not criticize him in public.

These four criticisms are severe. Don't use them if you want to continue your relationship.

Five Common Types of Inadequacy

A man compares himself adversely with all men when it comes to five critical attributes. He compares himself to the best man he knows in each category:

1. *His physical attributes.* He compares himself with the best of athletes.

2. *His mental attributes.* He compares himself with the sharpest thinker he knows.

3. *His moral attributes.* He compares himself with the most moral man he knows.

4. *His financial attributes.* He compares himself with the man who is most financially successful.

5. *His familial attributes.* He compares himself with the man who most displays strong family behavior.

Origin-Based Inadequacies

A man may feel inadequate about his origin or birth, including ethnic background, religion, race, appearance of family members, jobs, schools attended, or the home where he grew up. When you ask a man, "Where did you come from?" or "What does your father do?" or "Where were you born?" he may worry if he's from a third-world country, a shack, or a poor neighborhood.

If a man brags about his ancestry, don't let him look only to his illustrious ancestors and exclude the rest of his lineage. During the past four hundred years, each of us had more than one hundred thousand direct ancestors, excluding the effects of interbreeding. If you could trace his ancestry back to these hundred thousand ancestors, you'd likely find unsavory characters of various types. When he mentions one ancestor, ask him why he excluded the others. You might not be able to call him a son of a bitch, but you might be able to call him a great-great great-grandson of a bitch.

What should you do if the man criticizes *your* origins? You might feel that you have a low origin because of your birth, your immigrant status, or your family's caste. But you can turn this around, viewing your origin with pride of achievement. You are achieving your goals with perseverance; show delight that you have overcome any inadequacy associated with a lowly background! Take pride in your roots, as they've made you what you are today. You may be fortunate to have come from a small town or a foreign country where family values were so strong. You've come a long way for a small-town youngster or a child of immigrants!

Physical Inadequacies

Men are concerned with their physical inadequacies. Even a handsome man winces with any references to his size, age, weight, shape, build, hair, accoutrements, or dress. A man may feel physically inadequate because of his actual inadequacies, due to lack of physical acceptance by others, or because he's uncomfortable with his own body. The man's appearance is an especially good source of criticism because we do not see ourselves except as a reflection in a mirror, and this sight we usually scorn.

Your man might remind you that you are not a sought-after beauty. Let your fellow know that some men find you attractive, and that they view as an attribute the feature he sees as a flaw. Let him know that there is no universal beauty. You are more beautiful to some men than a beauty queen. Beautiful women have a difficult time marrying. Ordinary women marry with greater ease.

Financial Inadequacies

A man may attempt to diminish you by bragging about his wealth or income. If he does this, bring him down to size by provoking his own feelings of financial inadequacy. You might say, "You're so smart, I'm surprised you're not richer." Comment on the low financial return he receives on his assets, or their slow appreciation in value, or the excessive amount of taxes he pays.

A man who is hovering about the poverty line may cringe when you inquire what kind of car he drives, or where he bought his shirt, or where he lives. Even a very wealthy man is familiar with wealthier people and will feel inadequate about his worth. Most men compare themselves to the richest man they know, never making comparisons to the less fortunate. If John owns a hotel, he compares himself to Nicky who owns three hotels, while Nicky compares himself with Ron, who owns a large hotel chain. Use financial criticism only with a great deal of care. Criticize him only if he brags about his financial status.

Don't be concerned that *your* material goods are wanting. If he diminishes you financially, let him know that his wealth can be gone tomorrow.

Inadequacies in Education

Even a well-educated man realizes that there is much he does not know. Men are always concerned about being asked a question in public that they should know the answer to but don't. A man rarely feels adequate outside his field. Even in his field, he may not feel fully confident, since he may not know the subspecialties. Never let him think he is too knowledgeable for you. This should be the key inadequacy for you to use.

You may have gone beyond the limits of your formal education. There are more than a million books in print. It would take many lifetimes just to read the titles, never mind the contents. Each of us has read some of these books, and in this hodgepodge of knowledge, each of us knows something the other doesn't. If your fellow challenges you, say, "This is the third dumb idea you've expressed today" or "How could you, such an educated man, speak so poorly?"

Ethical Inadequacies

A man may be concerned with his ethics and those of his family. He may have secrets that would embarrass him profoundly if the public found them out. He may question whether his family has clean hands in achieving their present position in society. Did his father make shady deals? Is his brother on drugs? Is there an illegitimate child in the family? Use his sense of moral inadequacies if he is attacking your morals or ethics or is criticizing your family. Be proud of your family values, and take pride in what you've accomplished. Use this criticism for self-defense only.

Consequences of His Inadequacies

When you need to do so, make your fellow conscious of his feeling of being inadequate. Here are examples of inadequacies you might point out to him:

> His inadequate social behavior
> His lack of status
> His lack of table manners
> His short temper with his boss
> His lack of accomplishments

He may try to make you feel inadequate as a defense, though he might not believe his own words. Some men start this process, inciting the woman's inadequacies within herself, often to test her as a prospective mate. You might have to let him know of his inadequacies when you need to impress him with your positive attributes. Show spunk in defending yourself. Otherwise, he'll think you won't do a good job defending your future children and him from the outside world.

Removing Job Approval

When you are dating a man who is trying to impress you with the importance of his job, diminish his job to its appropriate level. Do not let him proceed as if his job is all-important. Say things such as:

> I'm sure there are other adequate people doing similar jobs.
> How many lives did you save today?
> When do you expect the Nobel Prize for your work?

Here are some other situations where you can incite the man's feelings of being inadequate by removing your recognition of what he has accomplished:

> If the man brags that he is a physician, point out to him that he lacks a law degree and is not qualified to enter the field of forensic medicine.
> If the man is a lawyer, tell him that he needs a CPA certificate to go with his law degree to be a tax expert.
> If he brags that he is wealthy—but *only* if he brags—make reference to people who are wealthier.

➤ If he is a capitalist, tell him he thinks too much like a social-
ist.

➤ If he is a doctor, tell him that he acts like a waiter.

You can diminish the value he places on himself by making
simple comments such as the following:

➤ You may be a professional, but you surely don't speak like
one.

➤ If you were two inches taller you'd be perfect.

➤ Your clothes almost match.

➤ You're acting childish.

➤ Pay attention when I'm talking to you.

When Your Man Is Arrogant

If you need to, you can highlight any and all of a man's inadequacies. This is the technique to use when he is particularly arrogant,
especially if he sharpens his tone of voice in speaking to you
challenges your uniqueness and importance, or becomes overly
critical and picky. You can also use this technique if he starts taking you for granted or shows any signs of boredom with you. At
those times, criticize. On occasion, challenge your man with
such phrases as, "Sure, you are Mister Universe," or "Yes, I
remember when you received an Oscar." Statements like these
can be used to revive his inadequacies and not frighten him off.

Constructive criticism generally is preferable to nonconstructive. If a man has been particularly arrogant or demanding, however, use nonconstructive criticism such as, "If you were a few
years younger you may have gotten that role."

Many women who are conscious of their own inadequacies are
afraid to criticize a man. The popular expression *You have no
room to talk* keeps them quiet. They fear that the men will turn
on them and devastate what little pride they have. When you
incite a man's inadequacies to the extent that they hurt him, he
will retaliate with nasty words of his own. Expect this natural

reaction and realize it means that you have successfully reached him. He may not mean the things he says when he is hurt; it's his way of saying "Ouch!"

Limit your criticism. If the man becomes convinced that you are out to destroy his ego, he will turn on you. You should not push him into a situation where his survival or self-importance is at issue. Even your own pet puppy dog will withstand a spanking or pain inflicted by you as long as it feels you are not planning its destruction. If it fears destruction, it will turn on you. So will the man.

Using the Man's Conscience

When you need to criticize a man, you can use his conscience as a basis for it. If he acts haughty or aloof, this technique can bring him down to earth.

Parents, bosses, spouses, relatives, friends, clergy, teachers, and enemies are the people who usually affect a man's conscience. They create in him a sense of underachievement. The individuals who formed your man's conscience make your man feel disappointing to them and to himself. They influenced his moral values and his views of himself, and he feels that he must account to them in some way. He attempts to act in a manner that pleases them even at the expense of his own happiness.

Answer these questions to determine who is affecting your man's conscience:

> Who is he not himself with?
> Who censors his ideas and conversations?
> For whom does he dress?
> From whom would he hide his emotional conflicts?
> Who would be concerned if he brought home a woman of a different religion or national origin?
> For whom does he tidy up his home more than usual?
> Who would be disappointed to see him poorly groomed?
> From whom does he hide his true financial position?

➤ Who are the people he would not ask for a loan even if he were starving?

➤ From whom would he hide his sexual history?

Listen to your man carefully and determine who is on his "conscience" list. Then, when you need to diminish him, bring up the unpleasant thoughts these people created. The following examples show how you can use a man's conscience. Here the man has a mother, boss, sister, and friend Jerry:

➤ What would your mother say if she saw you acting like this?

➤ Does your boss know how ignorant you are about that?

➤ Would your sister think as much of you if she knew you lost that client?

➤ Wouldn't Jerry like to know how little money you really made last month?

BALANCE PRAISE AND CRITICISM

By combining praise with criticism, you're saying, *I am good enough for you, but are you good enough for me?* Maintaining the proper balance is important.

In any relationship between two people, one person is generally superior in some ways to the other. This situation is analogous to a seesaw: When one party is riding high, the other is low. In the male–female relationship, one person cannot greatly outclass the other and enjoy a mutuality that leads toward a long-term relationship.

If you were a movie critic and claimed to like every film you reviewed, the public would lose respect for you. If you condemned every film, you would also lose credibility. To show that you have a discerning mind, you need to use both praise and criticism. You couldn't be an effective parent, teacher, executive, coach, friend, or spouse without knowing how to use both of these tools.

There are more negative words than positive words. You'll know two negative words for every positive word, and you might use that ratio when you speak. Stop that bad habit. Instead, use more positive than negative words in your general conversations. Your man should reward you with love as you repeat your compliments and the recognition of his uniqueness. Your friends will notice how happy you've become.

Determine Your Man's Ratio of Praise to Criticism

Learn the specific words of praise and criticism that will affect your man. Then apply the balance between praise and criticism that your man needs. You've discovered the extent to which your fellow received praise and criticism during his early years, as a teenager, and then as an adult. Most men view their family with fondness. These men are comfortable with a balance of praise and criticism that is comparable with their past experience.

Use the man's own experiences with the praise and criticism he received as a guide for dealing with him. In the normal case, take your cue from his parents. They most likely criticized him, but they accepted him with all his faults and virtues.

Some men rebelled against the level of praise and criticism they received when they were younger, especially if the praise–criticism ratio was skewed too greatly in one direction or the other. In that case, don't base your treatment of him on his prior experiences. Instead, base it on the ratio of praise and criticism he received from his good friends.

YOUR BEHAVIOR CAN WIN HIS LOVE

Are you a dud, who contributes nothing to the relationship? A fan, who praises and doesn't criticize? A nag, who criticizes and doesn't praise? Or a bitch, who does both? Of these four alternatives, bitchiness is the best; it keeps the man's emotions alive and makes him seek out your praise.

The Dud

If you never praise or criticize the man, he will view you as a dud, as a female wimp. You may think of refraining from criticism as a sign of love, as showing politeness or kindness, but he will see this restraint as a weakness. When criticism of him is appropriate, but you fail to criticize him, he is likely to be thinking one of three things:

1. You are too dumb to recognize his faults, and therefore are too dumb for him.
2. You are too insecure to point out his faults, and therefore are too cowardly for him.
3. He really is perfect, in which case he is certainly too good for you.

The Fan

We were taught to be nice, to not say unpleasant things, so that others would like us. "If you don't have something nice to say, don't say anything." Niceness gets little children a pat on the head by their parents or teachers, but doesn't get a man to love us, need us, and marry us. Put aside the childish rule of "niceness" and undertake conversations that incite a man's curiosity, passion, and desire. Do not fawn over your fellow or act like a fan. If you're too nice, you will eventually be taken for granted.

The Nag

The constant complainer or nag loses out by incessantly criticizing the man. If you criticize him more than his mother did, you're looking for trouble.

The Bitch

Think of the women you know who are most successful with men. These are the women who are demanding and complain to their men, but accept them nonetheless. You may think of these women as bitchy, but they have men flocking around them, men you lost by being nice. Sometimes you need to act bitchy to succeed with men. You may be too nice!

Show your man the high esteem you place on yourself by being hard to impress. Most men respond favorably to a woman who is hard to please, but only if she selects him. The man is honored to marry her! The man's general thought pattern about such a woman is this: *She has a high opinion of herself, therefore she must be someone special.* Or: *She has a low opinion of most people, and therefore, if she accepts me as her man, I must be someone special!*

The difference between the bitch, who succeeds with men, and the nag, who loses men, is that the bitch alternately tells the man he is wonderful and makes a fuss over him and dumps on him for his faults. Occasional bitching will keep them coming back for more, but constant nagging will lead to failure. Be a bitch, not a nag!

This phenomenon of men rejecting the "nice woman" is shocking to most women. They don't recognize that they're doing this very thing. They reject the "nice guy" who is always kind to them. These women view extreme kindness as a weakness, and view nice guys as wimps.

You may have a natural instinct to complain, but you have thwarted this instinct. Think of how you treat men in whom you have no interest. You are probably nasty from time to time, but they come back for more. Why? Because once in a while you show men some degree of acceptance. These men are very grateful for those moments. Yet when you truly like a man, you are always nice to him and he doesn't show interest. Stop being too nice to the man you really want.

WHEN HE CRITICIZES YOU

A man can make you feel inadequate. His comments can really hurt you. What should you do when a man points out your inferiorities or criticizes you? Don't show your emotions. Don't allow anyone to push you into reactions with either criticism or praise. Apply a middle course emotionally if you can. Let the outside world watch out for *your* use of criticism and your use of their inadequacies, not your fear of the world.

If your fellow criticizes you, wait until he finishes his criticism. You may want to respond in kind. Wait, and then ask him if that's all. When he says yes, respond in a manner comparable to his tirade against you, but don't expand the scope of the criticism. Conclude your tirade with a general acceptance of him such as "Despite your childish antics, I am stuck on you." You soon will teach him to vent his angers and forget them!

When you know you're going to lose your cool, try this strategy. Show your anger, but don't let him know what really caused the hurt. This is the safest approach for your own psyche. If he knows exactly what reached you, he can cause you real pain anytime he wants to. He may even say something very painful that will cause you anguish later. As you gain experience, though, it will become easier to control your own behavior and deflect his attack to areas of little emotional impact on you.

WHAT ABOUT ME?

Show pride in yourself. You need to feel that the man you love treats you as special and unique, and that he's unique or special to you. You should feel lucky to have each other, upholding each other's sense of happiness and pride. If your fellow doesn't show you how special you are, he's not your ideal mate. Move on.

chapter 9

Resolving Destructive Arguments

Arguments can happen during any relationship, even when you're in love, and even after you've met the man of your choice and are building a permanent relationship with him. An argument that isn't nipped in the bud with logical responses and self-control can end up in a fight. Try to resolve your disagreements before you reach the point of anger. Otherwise, it may be too late.

Since you want to resolve or evade bitter disputes with your fellow, you'll need to improve your arguing skills. You'll need to learn about the role of anger in arguments. Then you'll need to learn the techniques for responding to fallacious arguments. Your goal here should be to express your thoughts effectively while fostering your relationship. Winning—or losing—a specific argument is quite secondary.

I'll help you handle arguments appropriately. Resolving disputes with good logic will enhance his respect for you.

RESPONDING TO FALLACIOUS ARGUMENTS

Fallacies are misleading, deceptive, and erroneous statements that do not conform to the laws of logic. Fallacious statements influence our judgments and our lives if we believe them. The first step in handling destructive arguments is to recognize fallacies.

Once you learn how to recognize these fallacies, you'll notice that some individuals commonly rely on them in making everyday arguments, especially between a man and a woman. You'll learn to recognize fallacies and counter them when used against you. You'll be able to point out the errors in your fellow's reasoning and avoid making fallacies of your own when you argue. I'll help you use good logic instead.

Arguing at the Person

The most common fallacious arguing method is arguing at the person rather than addressing the specific facts under dispute. An argument is directed at the person if there is an attempt to discredit the individual personally, such as by calling the person a liar or by making other unfavorable personal comments.

Sandy and Harry are arguing about the purchase of a beach house. Sandy points out the merits of the purchase, and what it would mean to them. Harry, who lacks a good reason for rejecting the purchase, makes statements against Sandy instead. He argues, "You're just too lazy to drive to the beach." Sandy's response to this personal attack could be: "You're avoiding the issues by attacking me personally. What is the real problem you're having with the purchase?" She also might say, "You're not being objective, stick to the issues," or "Harry, what do you really think?"

Attacking the person rather than facing issues can often cause irreparable harm to a couple. If Sandy and Harry continue attacking each other, the end result could be hurt feelings or worse.

The following statements are personal attacks. Which of these do you recognize?

➤ You're too young to understand.
➤ If you're so smart, why aren't you rich?
➤ You've never been married, you can't give me any advice on marriage.

> ➤ How would you know? You don't know anything.
> ➤ No one would agree with you.
> ➤ You are behaving like a spoiled child.

Personal attacks are more than nasty commentary or criticism. They challenge the person's credibility just to win an argument.

Winning by Power

A second fallacious way of arguing is attempting to win an argument by power. Examples of this fallacy are when bosses win their arguments with employees because of their authority or police officers issue tickets to innocent drivers. When you were young, your parents won many arguments with you because of their authority over you. This is the "do it or else" argument. Traditionally, men tried to win arguments by using their financial power and women tried to win arguments by using their sexual power.

Here are some statements that reflect winning by power. Which of these do you recognize?

> ➤ Do it my way or find another job.
> ➤ Until you see it my way, sleep on the sofa.
> ➤ Mom knows what is best for her daughter.
> ➤ Keep this talk up and I'm leaving.

These winning-by-power assertions aren't really arguments. They're threats. You can't argue with a threat, but don't let your intelligence be insulted. Say, "You're not interested in hearing my thoughts, you're threatening me instead. Let's discuss this issue later when you're willing to put threats aside." Then postpone the discussion to another day when rational heads prevail.

Arguing Out of Ignorance

Also fallacious is arguing out of ignorance. Before space explorers went to the moon, some people argued that the moon was made out of cheese. No one was able to settle the argument with proof because no one knew the facts.

Many arguments between couples involve matters not subject to proof, especially arguments about their future plans or expectations. Predictions, superstitions, overly broad statements, and guarantees fall into this category, too.

Here are statements that indicate arguing out of ignorance. Which of these do you recognize?

> Many marriages end in divorce, so why bother getting married?
> If you break a mirror, you'll have seven years of bad luck.
> I'm sure he's saying that because he only wants to impress you.
> There's no better shampoo for your hair than Brand X.
> From the way you're carrying that baby, it'll be a boy.

You can respond to these arguments by stating, "Nobody knows," "Only time will tell," or "It's too soon to know."

Arguing Based on Popularity

Another common fallacy is arguments based on popularity, which use mob appeal rather than reasoning. Men make use of this fallacy in arguing, "The other guys are going to play golf, so I'll go, too." Women use this argument when they say, "Everyone likes the new mall. I'm shopping there, too." Children are masters at using this argument: "Julia got to go to the circus, why can't I?"

Here are some arguments based on popularity. Which of these do you recognize?

> All our friends have vacationed in Miami. We should go there, too.
> Everybody likes this pie. Let's buy it.
> Everyone knows she's a flirt.
> Mikey uses rah-rah sneakers, you should, too.

Respond to these arguments by stating, "I'm not going to let what someone else thinks determine my life." A simple "So what?" can be effective as well.

Arguments Based on Pity

Arguments may appeal to a sense of pity rather than reason. All too often, one person demands that the other person do something solely to make someone feel good, ease a pain, or satisfy someone else's wishes, even someone who might not be alive.

The following statements argue out of pity. Which of these do you recognize?

> Let her know that someone loves her, send her flowers.
> Let's go to the cemetery, it would make my poor mother very happy.
> In Dad's memory, please don't wear pink.
> I don't feel well. Can't you just agree with me this time?
> My dog died. Can I pay you next month?

Most of us are sensitive to another person's woes. When this argument is used against you, respond with, "That's a very sad story, but give me a logical reason to back your request."

Using Unestablished Authorities

Another fallacious argument is an appeal to an unestablished authority. These arguments are prefaced with "The doctor said so," or "I read it in a book," or "The newspaper said so," or "The teacher said so!"

These statements use unestablished authorities. Stop and think how often you have heard them:

> Dentists recommend brushing your teeth with Brand X.
> Doctors favor this pain reliever.

> This magazine article has the best diet.
> If it was good enough for my father, it's good enough for me.
> My friends think we should have a party.

For every unestablished authority's point of view, there's likely to be an unestablished authority with a diametrically opposed view. You can respond with an unestablished authority's view or simply attack the credentials of the authority. For example, you can ask, "What makes him an expert?" or "My dentist says Brand Y is better," "I read just the opposite in a magazine," or "My professor would never agree with that concept."

Positive Assertions

Positive assertions are a favorite fallacy of politicians. "Everybody needs Joe." "This economic crisis will end!" Politicians often make positive assertions without providing substantial backing for them. Avoid positive assertions unless you're certain of what you're saying. Strong statements do not make an assertion true. To avoid making erroneous statements, it's better to use *perhaps, maybe,* or *it may be so* rather than words like *yes* or *no*. Be very careful in your use of the words *always* or *never*. Use of either of these words doesn't consider the exceptions that might exist to your statement of fact.

When a man says to a woman, "You'll never succeed in your business venture," he's making a fallacious positive assertion. You avoid making such positive assertions when you say "People usually go to church on Christmas," rather than "People go to church on Christmas," or you say "You may be wrong" instead of "You are wrong."

Here are other positive assertions you may recognize. Stop and think how often you've heard these statements:

> She's the best doctor.
> This restaurant serves the best steak in town.

➤ You'll love this movie.

➤ I know you'll like my mother.

➤ I brought you something you'll like.

The simplest response to this fallacy is "Why are you saying that?" "Do you honestly believe that?" is another good choice.

Loaded Questions

Loaded questions are blatant fallacies. They are attacks that presuppose facts that aren't true. If you answer a question such as "Have you given up your evil ways?" with a simple yes or no, either answer would put you in trouble. Similarly, if a husband answers the question "Do you still beat your wife?" with either yes or no, both answers would put him in trouble. The questions are loaded because you haven't established that the precondition is true, such as "having evil ways" or "beating his wife." These questions are also called prejudicial questions because no matter whether you answer yes or no, you are prejudicing yourself.

Here are more examples of loaded questions. Which ones do you recognize?

➤ Do you still drink too much?

➤ Have you overcome your hatred for your mother-in-law?

➤ Did you ever confess to stealing her boyfriend?

➤ Do you still dye your hair?

When you are asked a loaded question, attack the premises. In response to "Have you given up your evil ways," for instance, you could say "I've never had evil ways, so how could I give them up?"

Advertisers use flattery as a variation of a loaded question: "As a connoisseur, you'll recognize this as a great wine" or "People in the know buy at Joe's." You might not be a connoisseur or a person in the know. You could sharpen your own wits and have fun by recognizing advertising that appeals to flattery. In fact, you and your mate might enjoy spotting the many appeals to flattery you see or hear.

AVOIDING FALLACIES

There is no simple method for avoiding fallacies, but you should guard yourself against them in your own reasoning, and expose fallacies used against you, especially with men you're dating. You don't want a date or mate to hide behind fallacious arguments and not reveal true feelings and thoughts. You should learn what a mate truly thinks and why. If you don't know a man well enough to predict and understand his reactions to issues important to you, you don't know him well enough to accept him on a long-term basis.

Your man may repeat his fallacious arguments. Now you're prepared for that challenge!

Your Verbal Response

When your companion uses fallacies in arguing with you, object to his fallacious arguments. Here are more responses that you can use in responding to fallacies:

> ➤ Why do you say that?
> ➤ What recognized authority agrees with that?
> ➤ You couldn't tell that to a judge.
> ➤ Who told you that?
> ➤ Who cares what our neighbors think?
> ➤ Why do you believe that?
> ➤ You say that because—?
> ➤ Darling, there is an error in your thinking.
> ➤ Hold on, there's a fallacy in your logic.
> ➤ You're avoiding the issues!
> ➤ By whose authority, your grandmother's?
> ➤ Pity won't work today.

You can respond to the fallacy in a formal manner: "Your argument is fallacious because you are arguing out of ignorance [or whatever fallacy applies]." Alternatively, you can make the point in more caustic language: "Please hallucinate somewhere else!" Do not allow fallacies to go unnoticed; they are an insult to your intelligence.

The Rules of Evidence

You can learn to argue against fallacies by using some of the rules of evidence. Learn to distinguish among speculative thinking, expert opinions, and people who know the facts.

If you were a judge listening to a case and an uncle testified that his nephew was twenty-five years old but the aunt testified that the nephew was eighteen, you'd be exasperated. You would want the best evidence, which might be the nephew's recorded birth certificate. Absent a birth certificate, his mother would be the better witness.

To save your time and patience, demand the best evidence as proof. Lawyers call this, naturally enough, the best evidence rule. Insist that your man and anyone else give you the best evidence.

Logical Responses

Insist that your mate answer the specific question you ask. Often, a question is responded to with another question; this allows the responder to evade the responsibility of answering. Imagine that you are a lawyer in a courtroom asking a witness a question. You would be surprised if the witness turned the tables on you and started to ask you questions. In fact, a judge must often say to a witness, "Answer the question you were asked." That should be your response when someone tries to make you the witness instead of the interrogator.

It's important that you have planned logical responses to emotional, amateurish arguments. When you argue, use solid reasoning. This will show men that you have a good mind. If you argue in this manner, your companion won't hold your arguments personally against you. He may be angry at "logic," but not at your personal viewpoints. His anger will pass and leave no resentments against you.

The use of fallacies and lack of true logic is rampant in ordinary conversation. There's no need to drive your fellow away by insisting that every word he speaks must be as accurate as if he were testifying at a trial. Do, however, insist on logic when you're arguing serious issues. For example, suppose your fellow says you are beautiful. Would you really want to challenge his statement with a question such as, "What authority are you basing your statement on"? If your fellow says "I'm taking you to the finest restaurant in town," would you really respond with "How can you say that? Have you been to all the restaurants in this town?"

Ostracization

The greatest error you can make when arguing with the man you love is to ostracize him. Ostracization has ruined many relationships. You are ostracizing your man if you exclude, elude, banish, hide from, or refuse to see or speak to him. When you ostracize him, the relationship will wither and die because you've lost the means to influence him.

Eventually, the man will not miss you as much as you thought he would. He may take refuge in his inner mind as an escape from you, or he might start to view other women as more desirable.

Don't permit your male companion to ostracize you. Seek him out, even if you must temporarily give up the argument. Never allow your parents, friends, or anyone else you love to lead you to ostracize him unless you want to end the relationship permanently.

ANGER MANAGEMENT

You and your man may get angry at each other from time to time. Anger is natural as long as it isn't frequent. The maximum frequency for anger depends on your upbringing and his; people from angry households usually have a greater tolerance for it.

Anger tends to be cyclical. Some people become angry every day, some every other day, some once a month. A buildup of frustrations or unfulfilled expectations often causes such anger.

Imagine going to a pay phone to make a call. The first phone takes your money and doesn't work. The second phone takes your money and doesn't work. The same thing happens with the third through the tenth and last phone. People with a lower threshold for frustration would become angry and start pounding on the third phone. People with a higher frustration threshold may beat on the eighth or tenth nonworking phone. In everyday life, some of us will have a shorter or longer fuse that ignites our anger.

Try to determine your mate's anger cycle. You'll then know if he's just reached his threshold for his cycle and must vent his frustrations, or if he's truly angry at you.

Creating Your Safety Valve

Your fellow may be angry or frustrated. Help him transfer or displace these feelings to a different planned or spontaneous event, creating a sort of safety valve for your man's occasional anger. Your man, no matter how well educated, intelligent, or even-tempered, might become annoyed at you without justification. Make sure there's something minor he can yell about. For example, leave part of your closet a mess. Your man won't complain about the slight mess, except when he's in a really bad mood. The messy closet area is a safety valve that helps him to blow off steam.

If you become angry at your boss, parents, clients, or other people you cannot successfully yell at, you may come home angry and yell at your family or kick the dog! Well, an angry man acts in much the same way. He's angry and will take his anger out on the nearest person or thing that he can. That could be you.

Become aware of his anger and recognize his need for release. Let him rant and rave about the event. You don't want his anger toward others to keep him from marriage with you. Be emotionally prepared for his anger so you aren't affected by what he says and don't become angry yourself or feel hurt by his complaints.

Is His Anger Directed Toward You?

One rule of thumb you can apply in your daily life is not to pay much attention to the bad mood that your man expresses just before dinner. He's hungry and will become angry more easily. After dinner, his mood should be stabilized. He'll also likely be cranky if he's tired and is pushed to activity, and he may display a bad mood if he's sexually hungry or exhausted. Pay more attention to the angers he displays in other circumstances, because those angers may be real. There's a difference between crankiness and anger.

Try to resolve your true disagreements before he reaches the point of heated anger. Otherwise, it may be too late. Anger is sometimes justified. You may have broken a promise or forgotten to do something important for the other person. When justified anger occurs in a relationship, it should be expressed or it'll fester and eat away at the affection you share. Let him get it off his chest and rant and rave. Your goal should be to never go to bed angry at each other. Saying "I'm sorry" can often normalize even a furious person.

If You Must Show Your Anger

Some arguments with your man might make you so angry that they will affect your behavior toward him. You may not want to talk to him, go out with him, or bed him. If you must, withhold other things, but never deny sex because of anger. Denial of sex weakens sexual exclusivity. He—or you—may go elsewhere to seek "sexual insurance."

An angry person often behaves in either a hostile or an indifferent manner. Your angry behavior can destroy your relationship if it's emotionally painful to the man, costs him money, or causes him a loss of self-respect. If you are angry to the point that you can't behave rationally with your companion, then blow off your anger by telling someone, such as a close friend, what is troubling you.

If venting doesn't help and you still feel like trampling your companion, then postpone seeing him for a week. Be sure to have set down a definite time to meet with him, however, or you may never see him again. Seven days without you may lead him into someone else's arms.

There are more steps to anger management. Try to carry on life as usual with him, even if you're angry. Still, in extreme cases, you may not be in full control of yourself and must do something nasty. The following strategies are preferable to fighting, but I don't recommended them for dealing with a man under normal circumstances:

> Refuse to call him for one day.
> Refuse to drive him somewhere such as to the airport to catch a flight.
> Refuse to make a telephone call he has asked you to make.
> Refuse to run an errand for him.
> Refuse to wear what he wants you to wear.
> Refuse to serve him a drink.
> Refuse to watch a TV show or movie he prefers and insist on your choice.

Excessive Pride Can Ruin Your Relationship

Pride causes havoc in a male–female relationship. Excessive pride is one of the primary reasons why relationships end. When you feel insulted by your man, you may want satisfaction through a humble apology, serious retribution, or an end to the relationship. Women sometimes make such statements as "He is not going to talk to me that way," or "I'm not going to let him get away with that!" This attitude is the beginning of the end of a relationship. You may be faced with the choice of letting go of your pride and keeping the man or letting go of the man and keeping your pride. Be glad you have the choice.

In situations where your pride is wounded, try pretending that you have an identical twin. As the twin, you won't suffer the wounds to your ego, won't have the hurt feelings, and can deal with the man on a more objective basis. This suggestion has kept more than a few women from dumping a man they realized they would regret losing.

When an Argument Becomes a Fight

An argument can overwhelm logical responses and self-control, causing a fight. A fight is a heated argument that has physical repercussions, whether someone storms out of the house, refuses personal attention over an extended period to punish the other, or worse, resorts to physical violence.

It takes two to fight! Avoid fighting if at all possible. Don't waste your time fighting! Take the difficult step of ending the relationship if you are fighting frequently. Fighting over every little thing is just a prelude to "We can't get along. We should split up." Usually fighting couples end up parting, and each person has lost time and misspent emotions. Don't waste your time fighting!

chapter 10

Developing Your Sexual Strategy

Congratulations on your success with men. You're dating men who are serious prospects for marriage and you're starting to bond with some of them. You may be fantasizing about having a sexual encounter with the fellow you select—but wait! Avoid having a sexual relationship with a man until:

> ➤ You've interviewed him for the job of husband.
> ➤ He's invested emotions in you.
> ➤ You've approved him.

Sexual intercourse is a natural consequence of a male–female love relationship. But make sure the timing is right.

I'll show you when to begin the sexual part of your relationship with the man you love. Then I'll help you determine how you can use his sex drive to your advantage. Later, I'll show you how to further develop your love relationship with him, and how sex can lead to marriage.

SEXUAL STRATEGIES

Stop now and examine your sexual strategy, both yours and your fellow's. As in all things, timing is everything. You're likely to lose the man for marriage if you have sexual intercourse too early in the relationship. But you're also likely to lose the man for marriage if you delay too long in beginning the sexual part of the relationship with him.

The woman who lays down her body too early misses the opportunity to develop the man's deep affection for her. She deprives herself of the man's curiosity about her. Consider the importance of curiosity: What do you suppose a man would pay for a nude picture of a woman he doesn't know? In comparison, what would he pay for a nude picture of a woman he knows as a colleague, friend, or neighbor? His curiosity and price would be greater for the picture of the woman he knew. The man's curiosity about any woman's body generally ends after they've had sex ten times.

In general, you should have at least a dozen dates with your man before lovemaking begins, assuming you're contemplating marriage with him. Make sure that these dates include more than thirty hours of conversation between the two of you. These dates can be short, such as meeting for lunch. Don't intentionally arouse him sexually with your clothing or conversation when sex isn't in the picture.

Facing Up to the Alternatives

One woman told me that she had sex with a number of men. She took pride in her abilities as a lover, but her relationships didn't go beyond sexual encounters. She never learned a man's thought processes, dreams, and ideals. This woman didn't bond with the men she dated and ultimately failed with them. What could she do in the future? Could this be your story?

Another woman told me that she has been "saving herself" for marriage. She viewed her continued virginity as an asset of increasing value, like a fine wine that improves with age. She, too, had failed with men. Could this be your story?

Most men want to marry a woman who is sexually competent, a woman who is "good in bed." The typical man reacts adversely to virginity in an adult female. But this man doesn't seek a woman with great sexual expertise, either. Avoid these two extremes to increase your marriageability. Develop your sexual competency without becoming a "sexpert."

The Virgin

A man usually does not appreciate virginity in an adult female any more than he admires a woman who doesn't drive a car, read, or swim. He desires competence from a woman in all these activities and many others.

If, at the outset of a sexual encounter, an adult woman tells her man that she is a virgin, he is likely to wonder why no man has wanted her before. If this is your situation, let him know that other men have wanted you, but that he is unique in being able to have you. This technique has its limitations, particularly if you're past your twenties, since most men recognize that there are limits to their uniqueness.

Most women find an adult male strange if he has never had sex. Men normally view virginity in an adult female with equal dismay. If a woman older than twenty-five is a virgin and insists on remaining one until she marries, she's likely to die a virgin.

The Sexpert

The "sexpert," the woman with sexual expertise, is often frightening to men. If you know a thousand and one positions and have used them all, keep this knowledge to yourself, at least in the beginning of a relationship. A man typically wants to believe that his knowledge of sex is at least as great as his woman's.

UNDERSTANDING HOW SEXUAL DEVELOPMENT HAPPENS

How important is sex to all of us? A great deal. We pass through three stages of sexual development to reach adult life: selfishness, monosexuality, and heterosexuality.

The first stage is selfishness or self-love, which begins at infancy. If you hand a rattle to a baby, the baby may smile with joy. If you try to retrieve the rattle, you would be amazed at the baby's tenaciousness in holding on to the toy. Selfishness continues for a number of years and diminishes in our early youth. It is, however, never extinguished, even in adulthood.

A child progresses from selfishness into the second stage, mono-sexuality. This stage is a predevelopment state before the sexual urge rises within us. Here, boys play with boys, while girls play with girls. If a boy plays with girls, his male friends call him a sissy. If a girl plays with boys, her female friends call her a tomboy.

The third stage is heterosexuality, the attraction to the opposite sex. So-called primitive tribes allow young adults to live in their own communal hut, freely cohabiting with whom they choose, and emerging from that communal hut when they've selected their one mate for life. Dating is our own society's ritual. Since you're reading this book, you should be at the third stage.

The sex drive often decreases later in life, causing this cycle to reverse. Monosexuality then replaces heterosexuality, and later selfishness replaces monosexuality. Look and see if your fellow is retreating into monosexual activities, such as participating in all-male events rather than those that welcome women. Such a man may be past the point of being available for marriage.

How Society Conditions Us

Sexuality is an essential natural function, beginning at birth and continuing into old age. Within a few hours of birth, almost every normal male baby has an erection and all normal baby girls lubricate (the female counterpart of erection). Yet society distinguishes sexuality from our other natural functions, such as respiration, digestion, and sleep. Social and moral pressures can damage or mortally wound our sexuality.

A youngster's mind is often filled with conflicts between natural desires and the rules of society. These conflicts create guilt and contribute to the personality that the person exhibits. These youngsters become adults who have secret desires and passions. They have fantasies and dreams, but fear telling others.

Historically, societies repressed females more strongly than males because of the female's risk of pregnancy. Even now, some women find it difficult to appear friendly, natural, and casual. Instead, such a woman must overdress her body and become cold and unapproachable. She might fantasize about lovemaking, but fears society might discover her thoughts. She might become miserable, seeking psychiatric help if she can get it. An honest and educated psychiatrist would help her see that sexual activity is a natural function.

A woman who fights off her natural sexual desires becomes repugnant to men. Her lack of sexual satisfaction brings on anxieties that cause unacceptable behavior to a normal male. She makes poor decisions because she suffers from a multitude of fears. Even a homely woman who enjoys sexual satisfaction radiates a warmth that makes her attractive to men. Just ask any married woman if men became more attentive to her after her marriage vows.

Our society frightens people against their sexuality. Guilt based on this oppressed sexuality is the basis of unhappiness that can last a lifetime. Sexual guilt does not have its origin in nature. Otherwise, guilt would be distributed equally among all cultures. We should instead recognize sexuality as a gift from nature that we can share with our mates. Move toward pleasure and away from pain during your lifetime. That is your ultimate reward. In the end, the amount of pleasure you receive will be your mark of success.

Determining Your Social Code and His

Your man at heart is a little boy. Even if he's tall and strong, he's programmed to follow his social code, which is lodged within his inner mind. If you transgress his social code, he'll pass you by for marriage. You have your own social code as well; if he transgresses your social code, then you'll pass him by for marriage.

For example, you might have had sex with a man before you knew his sexual standards. He might have consciously enjoyed the performance, but unconsciously disapproved of that activity. He might not marry you because of his inner mind's condemnation of you, treating you as unworthy despite his being the aggressor.

Determine at first instance the man's culture and morals. Ask the following questions of him in a normal conversation. Focus on the tone of his response, not just the response itself:

➤ Did your parents indulge in premarital sex?
➤ Is your sister a virgin?
➤ Did you ever see your parents in the nude?

If your fellow recoils in horror at merely being asked these questions, you can be sure that he is mired in prudery. If you're in doubt about where he stands, then ask him:

➤ When did you first masturbate?
➤ Do you watch porn?
➤ Have you paid for sex?

His answers are the keys to his sexual values. If he would reject his adult daughter or his widowed mother for engaging in sexual encounters, say no to his sexual advances. He has traditional anti-sexual values that can count against you if you have a sexual relationship with him before marriage.

Judge your man by the actions of his past with other women, not by what he says. Knowing his history, you should be able to predict with great probability what you must do to make him react favorably to you.

If your man asks you for an unusual sexual act, play it safe sexually by initially consenting only to acts that are generally acceptable. Place the burden of any deviation upon your fellow. If he asks for anything different, let him know that you have never indulged before. Let him convince you that this activity is natural.

Understanding the Male Sex Drive

Sex is a predominant thought in the mind of a normal man. His sex drive is second only to his drive for self-preservation. If the man is not immediately concerned about his survival, his thoughts turn to satisfying his sexual needs. A typical man will sleep with almost any female if there are no repercussions. If he's a sexually hungry male, he'll seek the nearest "restaurant."

The sex drive is an urge that has to be satisfied for a person to be physically comfortable. Someone in need of sex is likely to be irritable and fearful. Sexual tensions increase with each continuing day until sexual relief. This person becomes incapable of physically relaxing or concentrating, continuously building nervous energy.

Women as well as men need a sexual relationship. We all know of marriages where the wife is a screaming shrew, constantly criticizing her mate. She is an incessant nag, using her nervous energy to pick on him mercilessly. She may be suffering from a lack of lovemaking. A satisfying sexual encounter will help make her a cheerful person who loves life and radiates happiness.

A man might view a sexual encounter as his "reward." Such a man invests his time, money, and energy in his dates because he expects these sexual rewards. But all is not lost. If sex is *all* this fellow is interested in, he can go to any brothel and rent a body beautiful to do with as he pleases. The good news is that most men don't turn to prostitutes. Even better, it's a small percentage of men who seek sexual encounters as their sole reward. What a man really wants from a woman is her recognition that he is unique and special and who has good sex with him because of his uniqueness.

His Gift Is Sex

The mature male views his sexual activity as the greatest gift he has to offer to the female. Any rejection on your part sends a man's inner mind into a battle against you, forcing him to seek a woman who appreciates him and needs him.

In order to be happy, a man must feel that the woman needs him sexually. If she doesn't tell him how much she desires him, he will fear she's cold or not interested in him. Without her assurance that he's good in bed and greatly enjoyable, he'll feel rejected.

Don't judge a man sexually by his appearance. Nature is cruel and deceiving. The man who appears most virile and adequate often has a low sex drive. Conversely, the man who looks cool and sleepy is probably the temporarily satisfied sexual dynamo. If you rely solely on looks, you might be deceived as to his desires and capacities.

Teaching Him About Sex

Your man might not know the basics of female sexuality. Let him know that while the man travels steadily to climax, the woman needs more sexual stimulation and moves from hot and cold, usually needing more time than the man before reaching orgasm. He'll learn the crests and waves of your excitement. Teach him how to satisfy you, and offer to learn his preferences.

STARTING YOUR LOVE LIFE

Men have a panoply of sexual needs. A man who needs sexual satisfaction will welcome sexual performance on the first date. Another man will not hold it against a woman who makes love during their first date if his ego makes him believe that she has recognized his uniqueness. Still another man might be willing to wait, perhaps even until marriage. Some women claim that men want relationships with them only for sex. In fact, men want much more, and while most men will not stay with a woman who offers little or no sex, sex alone is not enough.

Unless your fellow has an enormous sexual appetite, postpone sex with him until you have heard most of his sexual history. The goal is to restrain him from pursuing a sexual relationship with you long enough to build his desires and yours. When he is so eager for you that you feel he cannot stop, that's the point to bed him. Every subsequent act should retain some of the intensity built up at the first encounter.

Before You Bed Him

You should know your man well before lovemaking begins. Don't look just to the number of days or months you have known him, but also to how well you know him. These are absolute minimum-threshold questions that you should be able to answer:

> ➤ How old is he?
> ➤ How old was he when he first had sexual intercourse?
> ➤ What is his religious background?
> ➤ How many times was he married?
> ➤ Why did the marriages end?
> ➤ Why did he choose his job?
> ➤ How popular was he with girls during his teenage years?

➤ How would he protect both of you from venereal disease?

➤ How would he protect you from unwanted pregnancy?

➤ What are his views about abortion?

Create Curiosity Before Beginning Your Sexual Encounter

Sex should begin when women and men both share curiosity, affection, and love. Give the man sufficient chance to develop sexual curiosity about you, since curiosity can normally sustain a relationship for about ten sexual encounters. But more than curiosity is needed over the long term, so make sure that the man develops deep affection for you as well. By building the relationship before lovemaking begins, you're assuring that he won't leave you after he satisfies his sexual curiosity.

When the man makes advances and you want to delay a sexual encounter, don't tease him or incite his passions. If he becomes too aroused and is not satisfied, he may be angry with you for teasing him to that point. Reject having sex, but not him.

To keep your man coming back to see you before you're having sex with him, indicate that you will have sex with him as soon as you know him better. Tell him that you like him physically, but don't want to rush into a sexual relationship. Say something like the following: "Every man I've dated wanted to take me to bed. What kind of wife would I make for you or any man if I had always allowed it?"

The man should believe that as you act with him, you have acted with others. Tell him that you want to make sure that he's as wonderful as you think he is. Be hard to impress, not hard to get.

It's sometimes to a woman's advantage to postpone the sexual relationship even longer. If a man has old-fashioned values, and was on the losing side in the sexual revolution, continue the delay if you can comfortably forgo sex. The longer he waits, the greater value he will place on the initial sex act.

Know a man well before you have sex with him to make sure he is a safe sex partner, recognizing that men, too, are seeking safe sex partners. If you insist that your man use condoms until you both are sure you can't infect each other, he should appreciate your caution and selectivity. If you want him to be tested for AIDS, offer to be tested yourself for his peace of mind.

If a man believes that a woman finds him desirable, he will not end a relationship with her solely because she delays sex for a while. The nonsexual beginning, from minutes to years, depends on the man's mores and sex drive. Build up your sexual worth by postponing your first sexual encounter until his anticipation of enjoying you is so great that the occasion is like a national holiday. But remember, holidays come and go.

Once a woman has sex with a man, his inner mind compares her to all the others he has bedded. This comparison may be a harsh one. An old-fashioned man might pass by this woman for marriage because she had sex with him too early. A modern man might pass by this woman for marriage if he views her performance as poor.

Sexual Compatibility

Sexual compatibility is an essential ingredient in marriage. In fact, lack of physical sexual compatibility destroys many marriages. We're horribly miseducated to believe that "one size fits all" when it comes to sexual partners. You won't even think about buying shoes unless you know their size and have tried them on. Sex, to my way of thinking, is at least important as a single pair of shoes. I treat each person as unique. This uniqueness includes sex organs!

Your First Sexual Encounter with Him

The sex act is an emotionally charged act. No wonder that it's one of a man's most important considerations for marriage. Make the first sexual experience with your prospective husband as intense and as unforgettable as possible.

Sexual Fantasy

You can intensify your first sexual encounter by realizing one of your fantasies or his. If you were to cook dinner for the first time for someone you wanted to impress, you'd likely ask, "What's your favorite dish?" and try to please your guest's taste. Imagine how pleasing sex would be if you fulfilled the other person's dreams. Here are two examples.

Sylvia discovered that Bob lives in the same house he lived in twelve years ago when he was a teenager. Bob's house abuts the high school parking lot. As a teenager, he'd have to walk each morning through the student parking lot where couples were making out. Bob developed late in his teenage years, and his classmates ridiculed him as a twerp when he walked by the more sophisticated kissing crowd. This memory was vivid and painful each time he glanced at the parking lot.

Sylvia decided to start the sexual part of their relationship on his birthday for added intensity. She told Bob to dress in jeans because she was going to pick him up and drive him somewhere special but casual. She rented a vintage car from Bob's high school years, gathered CDs of the then-popular songs, packed a picnic basket with their favorite foods, dressed in her old high school outfit, and went to pick up Bob. Can you guess where she took him? To the parking lot right next door where she proceeded to seduce him. Since that occasion, Bob has smiled every time he's seen the parking lot.

Larry mentioned to Leslie that he had a fantasy of seeing a beautiful woman standing at the top of the stairs in a white negligee, holding a lit candle. This woman descends the steps slowly; when she reaches Larry, she blows out the candle and falls willingly into Larry's arms. Leslie had no problem setting that scene for their first time together.

If acting out his fantasy is simple, why not do it? If you've missed the opportunity to use fantasy to enhance the first time, you can still use it to intensify a later encounter.

Enhancing Your Sexual Encounters

Some clothing is more erotic than none at all, so excite him with various stages of dress and undress. A gesture such as loosening his tie, slipping off his shoes, or unbuttoning his shirt will create a positive mood. Make the removal of clothing a playful art. Comment on how you enjoy his hairy chest, or strong arms, or big hands. Sexual teasing is appropriate now because it is going to lead to sexual satisfaction.

On rare occasions, you can enhance a sexual encounter by evoking anger, but not fury, before the sex act. You've probably heard of couples who have terrible fights and then make up and have the best sex ever—what's called make-up sex. If you incite one sense, you may awaken the others. If you tease the man to anger, you may arouse him sexually as well. He will believe that there's something special about his passions for you. Do not use this technique except in rare instances, though, because the fight could get out of control.

Plant the idea of lovemaking in your man's mind early in the day. That way, when he sees you in the evening, his desires for you have long been awakened. Expressions such as "Honey, I can hardly wait to enjoy you" will spark him. Keep him in anticipation just for a few hours, making his passions greater. He'll believe that you are especially desirable.

Establish a ritual of pleasures both before and after lovemaking. Buy him a robe or lounging outfit if it'll add to his comfort, and provide him with the toiletries he uses. Soft music, dim lights, and an inviting living room and bedroom will create warm and comfortable feelings. Use everything at your disposal to enhance the moment.

Bedroom Manners

Here are tips for improving your bedroom manners and enhancing the sexual aspects of your continuing relationship:

- ➤ Don't destroy romantic illusions. Give him the option of undressing you. He may prefer to undress you slowly since that is more erotic.
- ➤ If you are fertile, use birth control that's pleasant for him. Don't expect him to use a condom, unless disease prevention is your primary concern or his. Condoms may dull his senses too much.
- ➤ Don't expect him to sleep on crumpled sheets or the wet spot. Fix up your bed!
- ➤ Give him his own new toothbrush. There's a limit to intimacy!
- ➤ Never complain about his sexual performance, unless you're willing to end the relationship. Don't ridicule the size of his penis or compare him unfavorably to other men.
- ➤ If he has difficulty getting or maintaining an erection, assure him that you care for him and that he will perform beautifully when he's more relaxed.
- ➤ Be considerate before sex and after.
- ➤ Don't store trinkets or money in your underwear.
- ➤ If he must leave before recovering his energy, offer him sweet snacks.
- ➤ Invite him back.

Bedroom Attitudes

Your bedroom attitude can help make you a superior lover. One pleasurable reminder of childhood that follows us into adulthood is the concept of play. In adulthood, this concept is demonstrated most clearly in bedroom attitudes. The bed should be the adult playpen. Your motto should be "Let's have fun." The atmosphere should be relaxed, sensual, and inviting. Your bedroom should look as if you're anticipating him with joy.

The best way to arouse a man is to be aroused yourself. Whatever feeling you convey will be contagious. Words cost nothing, yet they create any mood you choose in the mind of the man.

Since you've already listened to your man tell you about his sexuality, you should know what to avoid sexually. You will learn to not override your man's sexual cycle.

Some women refuse to speak to or cuddle with the man after the sex act. They don't know if he's satisfied or not. These women later sit in bewilderment as to why their affairs are short.

Praising Sexual Performance

Praise is the last and most important part of the sex act. Praise his sexual performance when appropriate and expect him to praise yours. If you spent time preparing a scrumptious meal for a man and he offered not even the slightest inkling of enjoyment, gratitude, or appreciation, chances are you wouldn't invite him for dinner again.

A man seeks reassurance about his sexual performance from the beginning, because the sex act is rarely passive for him. Once he has exhausted the excess sexuality of his early youth, he views his time and energy as valuable. The better you make him feel about sex with you, the higher you'll rate with him. Saying, "Honey, you're terrific," can make the difference in your relationship. If sex has been unsatisfactory over an extended period, you may be wrong for each other. But if it's good, tell him so.

After Me—Make It Coffee or Tea

A man behaves quite differently when he's satisfied than when he's sexually hungry. After sex, he may not be as considerate. If you're eager to ask a favor from him, or want to press an issue that will require his giving in, ask him before he's sexually exhausted.

After intercourse, the man will have little energy left. Let him sleep if he wishes. Then be prepared to revive him with coffee, sweets, and appetizing snacks. When your man achieves sexual satisfaction early in the day, he may be exhausted for hours. If you don't revive him, you may find yourself spending the day with a grouch. If you have sex at night, his body naturally recovers energy in sleep. By morning, his need for you is returning and he will be up to par.

Sex and Your Period

Yes, you can have sex with your man during your menstrual period, but avoid this if it's your first encounter with him. Be sure to follow these tips:

> Let the man know you're having a period.
> Give him a chance to postpone sex. Even today, some men refrain from sex during a woman's period.
> Most men will have sex with a woman during that time of the month; some men avoid oral sex during those days.

Determining Sexual Cycles

After you initiate your sexual life with your man, you can use his sexual cycle to your advantage. Men are sensual animals. They suffer from the same desires, passions, and vanities as do women. Sexual needs differ in degree from one man to another. One man may require sex a number of times every day for his well-being. Another man will be completely happy indulging once a month or less often. The man with a great need for sexual intercourse will suffer the same irritability after one day of no sex as the second man would suffer after several months!

You can determine your man's natural sex cycle. This is easy to do. Then you should consider whether his sexual cycle and yours mesh well together. To find the outer limit of his cycle, just say, "Honey, we should wait until tomorrow." There will come a day that he will refuse to postpone sex any longer, or he will become very argumentative over the postponement. The time period that elapses between a mild acceptance of delay and a complaining reaction indicates the outer range of his true sexual needs.

Use the reverse technique to find the inner limit of his sexual cycle. Initiate frequent sexual contact and increase the frequency until he refuses sex. Then you'll know the other limit of his sexual cycle. You'll also have an irritable man on your hands until he recovers.

One smart woman wanted to determine her fellow's true sexual cycle. She suggested that they not see each other for ten days, but asked him to call her if anything came up and he wanted to see her. He called the third day, and she had her answer!

For optimum advantage, keep your man on his sexual cycle. Any period of time from several times a day to once every few months is normal. Occasionally stretch the cycle a day or two to build up added intensity, or reduce the cycle to diminish the risk that he will wander, particularly if he is going on a trip without you.

Once you learn your man's sexual cycle, use this knowledge to your advantage. These are two different strategies you should consider:

1. Keep the man a little bit hungry for sex with you. He'll keep coming back for more. But don't keep him too sexually hungry or he'll go elsewhere.
2. Keep the man very fully satisfied so that he'll have neither the energy, inclination, nor desire to look elsewhere.

Sexual Frequency

Your fellow judges what's normal based on his own needs. You'll lose your fellow if you continuously exhaust him sexually. He'll dismiss you as a nymphomaniac if your sexual cycle is higher than his and you press him for sex. But he'll dismiss you as frigid if your sexual cycle is lower than his and you deny him sex. He judges what's normal based on his own needs. If it becomes difficult for him to keep you satisfied, he will feel inadequate and pass you by. If it becomes difficult for him to achieve his own satisfaction, you will also be passed by.

The human body cannot overextend sexual energies without suffering consequences. Too much sex brings on irritability, indolence, depression, and even suicide. A wife who is oversatiated may become a slob, and her house may become a pigsty. Too little sexual activity can have even worse consequences.

Measuring Sexual Energy

Sexual energy is analogous to an electrical force. A battery has a positive and negative pole, each emitting a charge. If you make contact between the poles, you create sparks. If you maintain the connection, you'll exhaust the battery.

When a couple makes physical contact by holding hands, kissing, or petting, they're slowly discharging their sexual energies. Clothing functions as "insulation." The sex act, in contrast, discharges the flow of sexual energy quickly and exhausts the parties.

I once overheard the mother of a young woman say to a friend, "My daughter and her boyfriend are having sex." The other lady was surprised, and asked, "How do you know that?" The first mother answered, "They no longer hold hands or reach out to touch each other." She was a smart mother. She realized that the couple no longer needed a slow sexual energy discharge; they had achieved a rapid discharge through the sex act.

If you are skeptical about the "sexual energy" flow from body to body, wear rubber gloves when you hold hands with a man. See what effects do *not* occur! Since sexual energy is like an electrical force, we must realize that there are different rates of discharging this energy, and each has its value and pleasures.

Some people lack the complete satisfaction that comes from snuggling with someone continuously over many nights. This satisfaction comes from the continuous contact or rubbing against another body over an extended period of time. It is one body enjoying the mere warmth of another. For most couples, snuggling is one of the most rewarding aspects of marriage.

AVOIDING FOUR EGREGIOUS ERRORS THAT WOMEN MAKE

I've come across four specific errors that adult women make in sexual relationships. Each one alone can significantly decrease the woman's chance for happiness:

1. They establish a long-term relationship without sexual activity.
2. They engage in sexual activity without a commitment.
3. They deny sexual activity, using it as a weapon.
4. They act like a prostitute.

1. Don't Establish Sexless Relationships

A normal fellow is looking for sexual activity with his woman as part of his relationship. He expects that your relationship will become sexual. If your relationship with a man continues to be nonsexual after an extended period of time, beware. This man might have too low a sex drive to keep you happy or might not be heterosexual.

2. Don't Engage in Sexual Activity Without a Commitment

Sex without a commitment is the wrong way to lead the man of your choice to marriage. If marriage is your goal, the fellow you're dating casually could be wasting your time. Even when you give your all to a man, he might not cherish your body and rush you off to the altar. In fact, some men might even be happy to swap you for another woman. Your goal, then, is to secure that commitment from him. If he doesn't speak of the future with you in it, move on. Timing *is* everything!

3. Don't Deny Sexual Activity as a Weapon Against Him

Once you have sex with a man, don't use denial of sex as a weapon. Sexual denial, like the hydrogen bomb, is too powerful to be used as a weapon except in the most extreme circumstances. Some women treat their sexual activity as a commodity. They give men samples and then withhold sex until the man commits. Their idea is that the man will know what he's missing. He'll suffer more, and want her back in bed sooner. Don't do this.

Don't deny sex to him to win an argument or get a gift from him. Don't even hint at withholding sex to have your way! A man will feel that if you would deny sex to him as his lover, you'd be even meaner as his wife. Sexual activity is a primary consideration in marriage for a man. Any threat of withholding sex destroys his thoughts of marrying you.

If you are ill or are otherwise unable to perform, let your man know the specifics. If you don't tell him what's troubling you, he's likely to think that you are withholding lovemaking. Don't just tell him that "I have a headache" or "I don't feel like it tonight." Let him know that you are in trauma over the death of a relative, you are suffering severe menstrual cramps, or you have an earache.

Sexual exclusivity brings with it responsibilities for the other's satisfaction. The person who doesn't need sex needs to convince the partner to forgo sexual satisfaction. If either of you denies sex to the other without a good reason, the other will be frustrated with the relationship, and may begin to look elsewhere.

4. Don't Act Like a Prostitute

Some women are prostitutes at heart. As I've mentioned previously, they kid among their friends that it would be great to have a rich old man with one foot in the grave and the other on a banana peel. Men find this idea repulsive. If you don't want to appear as a parasite or prostitute, lay your body down to him only after you're willing to share your other prize possessions. If a man can enjoy your body but not drive your car, he'll think the car is worth more. Don't expect or accept lavish entertainment or gifts. If you expect the man to pay for the pleasure of your company, he's likely to view you as a prostitute rather than as his future wife.

BEFORE MARRIAGE

After your relationship is secure, consider building a togetherness immersion period or, as an alternative, start living together.

Immerse Yourselves

If you can't live with your future husband, do yourself and him one favor: See to it that you have a one-week immersion period with him. Be together for at least one uninterrupted week, twenty-four hours a day. Be in contact with the outside world, but spend as much time alone as you can. You'll know whether you want him on a permanent basis after only one week of immersion. Problems that could develop in your future marriage will surface that week. This one-week immersion should give you the insight you need to determine if your future should be together.

Living Together

Should you live with a man you are planning to marry? The answer is definitely, positively, yes. But there are exceptions, depending on the circumstances. Some men are so old-fashioned, so traditional, so overly religious, or from a different culture with a different set of values than yours. Before you marry him, reexamine whether such a person can be a suitable mate for you. If you make an issue of living together, you may lose him, but you may be better off.

The best surprise after marriage is no surprise. Use the living-together portion of the relationship as the final step in the process of selecting your ideal mate.

Benefits from Living Together

Lovemaking is only one benefit from living together; the primary benefits are nonsexual. Use this opportunity to see how you and your potential spouse get along together in close confinement. See how you share household bills and household chores as well as responsibility for decision making.

Most important, use the living-together relationship to discover your future spouse's personal habits. These are some of the questions you should be able to answer about your future spouse before you make the final decision to marry:

> What are his best times of the day? His worst?
> What is his favorite time for dinner? For lovemaking?
> Does he have difficulty sleeping?
> Does he snore? How loudly?
> Does he have a late-night snack in bed? Does he leave crumbs?
> What time of the day does he shower? Does he enjoy showering with you?
> Does he hog the bathroom or squeeze the toothpaste in the

middle of the tube? Are the hairs in the sink driving you to drink?

➤ Is he on the phone at all hours with his friends, family, and colleagues?

➤ Does he decide to do exercise or perform religious rituals at times you consider inopportune?

➤ Does he treat two-thirds of the bed as his turf? Or seize the blanket for his exclusive use?

When You Live Together

Can living together work against you for marriage? It can, if it starts too soon or continues too long. A relationship peaks and then plateaus. If this happens before marriage, you both will be settled in, and the impetus for marriage will be gone.

When people live together for many years and then marry, these marriages often don't last. These relationships have peaked and plateaued long ago, and may well be on the decline. The couple may try to use a marriage ceremony to save their relationship, but it's usually too late.

Sexual behavior rarely changes significantly after marriage, in terms of either frequency or satisfaction. If you haven't established a pleasurable sex life with your partner before marriage, don't necessarily expect a happy sex life afterward.

A premarital relationship is important for the woman, for she needs to assess the man's actions. He may be able to hide his true behavior when you're dating, but not when you're living together. He might be talking a good line, but his actions might be quite different. Use the living-together relationship to find him out.

Living together loses many of its benefits if the couple avoids chores and potential conflicts. Be yourself when you live together, and encourage your partner to do so as well. Confront daily life together, head-on.

chapter 11

Preparing Him for Marriage

Now we've come to the final step: moving your relationship toward marriage. But be careful here. Before you take this step, be sure the man you select is the man of your choice.

TEACHING HIM TO BE A HUSBAND

Men don't start out as husbands. They must be taught. Here are ten techniques you can use to show him that you are beautiful, intelligent, and his ideal mate, and that you need each other for happiness. Use these skills to make his relationship with you an unbreakable habit. Implant these ideas in his mind and bring these ideas to fruition.

1. Association

The mind can learn to associate two unrelated events, such as associating the serving of food with the hearing of a bell. A Russian scientist by the name of Pavlov did just that. He rang a bell whenever he fed his dogs. Later, when he just rang the bell, the dogs salivated because they expected food.

Use this association technique in your relationship with your fellow. Here's how:

➤ Let your man associate a song with a pleasurable moment with you.
➤ Let him associate a pleasurable color with a specific effect he enjoys sharing with you.
➤ Let him associate an outfit with an event that you both enjoyed, such as a sunset, the beach, or the mountains.
➤ Let him associate an erotic tone of voice with a mood or memory you both enjoyed.

If you consistently wear the same perfume or cologne, the man will associate the fragrance with you. If he smells this fragrance when you're apart, he will think of you. Similarly, if the two of you have your own song, he will think of you whenever he hears it. Light a candle every evening you make love to your mate. Just seeing the candle will increase his sexual interest in you.

Beware of negative responses, however. Your fellow might be similar to bears in the Russian circus. The circus conditions bears into dancing by means of hot stones and a fiddle. The bears are led onto hot stones and must hop from paw to paw to keep from being burned. As the bears are hopping, a fiddle is playing. Later, fiddle playing without the hot stones is sufficient to send the bears dancing. The bears associate the music with their burning paws. Your fellow might act like these bears to a number of "fiddles" or to the words you say. Avoid that "bear dance."

2. Intensity

Intense experiences teach quickly. A child who is bitten by a dog may later be fearful of dogs and may even be frightened by a picture of a dog. Any intense event leaves us with an emotional response to the people, places, or objects involved. Use an intense pleasurable response to work your way into his heart. When he does something pleasing that you'd like him to repeat, overreact in some special manner. Jump up and down, hug and kiss him, or shriek with pleasure. That's much more memorable than a thank-you. He'll repeat his action often enough that it becomes a habit with him. Surprises create intensity. A pleasurable big surprise might last forever.

3. Repetition

Make note when others compliment you. Let your man know that others tell you that you have beautiful hair, or a good mind, or a keen sense of humor. Tell him, "I feel pretty." Mention whatever features he responds to favorably.

Advertisers use slogans, mottos, and theme songs to evoke repetition. If an advertiser is fortunate, its clients will start humming its slogans. If you're really clever, develop a slogan or motto regarding your relationship, just as clubs and organizations use slogans to unite their members. Repeat the slogan whenever you want to remind him that you're a couple; work your "theme" into activities you share, presents you give him, notes you leave in the morning. ("It's you and me against the world," "We've only just begun," "We're in this together," "Together forever" are a few examples—but the best one will come out of your own experience.)

4. Rewards

Society conditions you by rewarding you for your behavior. A seal performs for the reward of a fish, a monkey for a banana, a squirrel for a nut, and you and your man perform on the job for paychecks. Reward him for his positive behavior toward you. Give him a superbig hug, smile, or kiss. If he does something nice, reciprocate! He'll repeat his action often enough that it becomes a habit with him. Do not use sex as a reward, however, just as you should never withhold sex as punishment if you want your relationship to be exclusive.

5. Praise

Men respond to praise. Every time your man does something you like, give praise. Here are some examples:

> ➤ You have a good head on your shoulders.
> ➤ You look great!
> ➤ Your hands are so comforting.
> ➤ Your eyes always sparkle.
> ➤ To know you is to love you.

Words are ideal, for they can be given anytime, anywhere, and without cost.

6. Commands

A strong voice with a commanding tone gets results. A bellowing "How could you do that?" or "Stop that" to something you dislike or "Fantastic!" or "Do it again" to something you do enjoy gets an immediate response.

7. Sweet Demands

Preface your demands with "Honey, you should" or "Please, darling." Saying "Honey, you should cut the grass Saturday"—especially if you start a few days before the lawn needs cutting—will get the grass cut on Saturday. You could, if you wanted to, use this approach: The first few days, you could say "Please darling, bring me my slippers"; on the fourth and fifth day, you say "Darling, bring my slippers." On the sixth day, it's "Bring my slippers," and on the eighth day, it's a snap of the fingers and "My slippers." This man won't even realize that he is responding to sweet demands.

8. Exhaustion

We are especially susceptible to suggestions when we're exhausted. If you tell your man at 6:00 P.M. that you are lovely, perhaps by repeating a compliment you received from someone else, he may have the mental energy to fight off this thought. At 3:00 A.M., his resistance is lower and he may not be able to reject your claim to loveliness. You could then let him know that you are lovely, good, and desirable. Use this time to implant the idea of your importance to him and the thought that you would be a perfect wife. This is the time to reinforce your sales pitch, which I'll discuss later.

9. Moods

A man can learn love and happiness with you. Your moods affect his behavior. If you radiate happiness, he will have a sense of joy. If you feel pleased with yourself, he will feel joyful about having you as his mate. If you appear happy whenever you're with him, he'll feel welcome and wanted by you at all times. Knowing he brings you joy will keep him by your side.

10. Example

One of the best ways you can teach a man to be a good husband is by being a good wife. Start this process before you're married·

- ➤ By having your mutual welfare at heart.
- ➤ By encouraging each other.
- ➤ By sharing problems and their resolutions.
- ➤ By keeping confidences.
- ➤ By maintaining positive attitudes about your relationship.

CONDITIONING

Conditioning is the most powerful tool you can use to control your man's behavior and lead him into marriage. You do so by implanting ideas such as marriage in his mind and developing them.

Conditioning is the process by which habits are formed; it establishes our culture, attitudes, morals, religious beliefs—our whole way of life. We aren't usually aware of the way in which we've been conditioned, but it happens constantly from advertisers, psychologists, the military, parents, schoolteachers, friends, and other "friendly" persuaders.

When a baby is born, his or her mind is a clean, blank slate. From that moment on, this beautiful slate is imprinted or conditioned. Some conditioning is beneficial, such as learning to brush our teeth, wear safety belts, and celebrate holidays. Sometimes, however, a baby is saddled with fears, phobias, superstitions, fairy tales, and idiotic customs. You may see some of this conditioning in your man's present behavior. A horrible thought!

Many of us have been conditioned into religion, customs, caste systems, blind patriotism, values, occupations, prejudices, and other beliefs. Men condition countless women to do all sorts of unpleasant tasks. Conversely, some women have conditioned their men to be their beasts of burden. We even can be motivated into seeking goals that in reality would make us unhappy if we ever reached them. For your own mental strength, make a list of what is natural for you to do and what you need to be happy. Then do not allow anyone to keep you from achieving your aims.

Your Own Conditioning

Bad conditioning may be adversely affecting your own behavior, keeping you from happiness. You may be prejudiced against certain types of men or certain professions. You may have fears of changing your lifestyle or even simply changing locations. If you have these fears or prejudices, you are conditioned into a rut.

You may not recognize the extent of your conditioning or how it affects your relationship with your man. Do you expect him to put the toilet seat down? Well, that's conditioning, because it isn't the natural order of things. It could be a no-win proposition for him, causing resentment against you. If you always urinate sitting down rather than standing over or straddling the toilet bowl, you do so because of your conditioning, too. Bear in mind that toilets differ across the world, and almost everyone is most comfortable with what they know.

Conditioning a Man into Marriage

Men implicitly accept the image of women that they observe in the media. This fictitious concept of an ideal companion lurks in their mind. In some instances, the man's mother and others augment and foment this image of an ideal companion, keeping the man unhappy by pointing out flaws in his dates. This situation makes it necessary for you to condition men to accept thought patterns that create a good relationship.

A man often seeks a woman for fun, amusement, companionship, sex, and other pleasurable reasons besides marriage. If you ask your married male friends if marriage was the reason they began dating their wives, very few would say yes.

The man's mind is fertile soil. All you need to do is plant the seed of a thought, and water it now and then; his imagination will expand it. Plant in his mind the concept that he will marry you. A simple phrase—"We make a good team" or "You and I deserve each other"—is a good beginning.

A marriage is not made overnight. It's more than a license to have sex. It's a gradual closeness of two people who feel married because they are bound together by mutual interest, need, love, and affection. At this point, it's often to their advantage to legalize their relationship.

Removing Superstitions and Prejudice

Superstition and prejudices that conditioning brings can destroy the possibility of a successful marriage. I'm talking about actions that are not based on truth. Replace these superstitions and prejudice with sense. These are some examples of the superstitions and prejudices you may have learned in the marriage context, but have no foundation in fact. Regrettably, some people believe them heartily.

> ➤ June is the only month for weddings.
> ➤ An engagement ring should be a diamond.
> ➤ A wife shouldn't let her husband see her in her wedding dress before the ceremony.
> ➤ A veil is essential to the wedding ceremony.
> ➤ Don't marry on Friday the thirteenth.
> ➤ Wear something old, something new, something borrowed, something blue.

Don't push your fellow into following these myths—and don't following them yourself.

Learning Love Behavior

Most of us have an image of what makes up love behavior. The problem, though, is that love behaviors differ between people. You might view getting breakfast in bed as romantic, but he may associate it with illness. You might clean up his room and wash his dirty dishes out of love for him, but he might think that the message you're sending to him is that he's sloppy and unable to pick up his own mess. You're not going to know his love behavior through osmosis. Instead, learn his love behavior through your experiences with him, and ask him about his experiences when growing up, especially how his mom treated him.

CREATING INTERDEPENDENCE

Before you started your relationship, each of you lived totally independent of the other. Now both of you should be happier because of your mutual companionship. The more the two of you share your talents and strengths, the stronger the relationship becomes. Interdependence is the culmination of your personal development. Consider these three steps to personal maturity: dependence, independence, interdependence.

From our earliest beginnings, we were dependent on others, especially our parents. Most of us eventually strove for, and attained, independence. We proved to the world, and to ourselves, that we could survive and thrive on our own. Now we can use the inner strength we developed from achieving independence while regaining the earlier joys of dependency. Interdependence is the key to self-fulfillment.

The successful woman generally prides herself on her independence. She is likely to believe that she can satisfy most, if not all, of her own needs. She often provides her own food, shelter, and entertainment. In fact, if she wants children, she may even have considered single motherhood. If she wants total independence from men, surely that has cost her marriage.

Interdependence

The key to mutual love is interdependence—your need for your fellow and his need for you. Your relationship with your fellow will thrive only if he meets your needs and you meet his. Need, in fact, is one of the most important facets of love. People rarely love a person unless they need that person for a sense of well-being.

Reciprocity in love—not in specific actions—is what's essential. Don't marry a man if you can't meet his needs. Perhaps more important, don't marry a man who doesn't meet your needs.

Prepare your own list of what you really need in life. Here are two lists of questions that will help you identify and specify your physical and emotional needs. Use these lists as a starting point, modify them to reflect your own situation, and then decide if your fellow is right for you and whether you are right for him.

Never assume that your fellow feels what you feel and shares your needs. Ask him instead.

Physical Needs

➤ How much sex do you need to be satisfied, to feel comfortable and relaxed? Is this level of sexual activity compatible with his needs and capacities?

➤ What material goods and services do you require? Include clothing and household help. How will these needs change when you're married? Have you asked him about your expectations and his after the marriage?

➤ What are your needs for rest and physical exercise? Are you much more energetic than he is? Or more lethargic? Do you have sufficient energy to carry out your usual daily tasks, or will you be counting on his energy to help you? How much care does he need?

➤ Where are you both planning to live once you're married? Who's going to find a place to live, care for your home, and pay the mortgage? Have you asked him what he thinks?

➤ How much personal time do you need to keep yourself happy? What about your fellow? Does he really know you as you truly are? Do you really know the true him?

➤ What foods will you cheerfully eat? Could you deal with his eating patterns, or would you resent not having your usual fare?

➤ How much sleep do you require to feel your best? Will your need for sleep or his be a problem? Could you sleep with the light or the television on, or must there be total quiet and darkness? Is he an early riser? Or are you? Does his sleeping pattern match yours?

➤ What home entertainment activities do you enjoy? Do your preferences irritate him? Do his activities annoy you?

➤ How often do you like to socialize? Do his plans conflict with yours?

➤ What level of cleanliness and order do you expect in your future home? How are the responsibilities to be shared? What does he think?

Emotional Needs

➤ Are you both angered by the same things and to the same extent? Will you feed each other's angers, or help each other cope?

➤ How well matched is your sense of humor to his? Can it help you over the rough times? Will you resent his capacity to laugh? Will he resent your joviality?

➤ How much ego bruising does each of you get on the job? How much ego stroking will you need from each other?

➤ What are the things that make you feel guilty? Will he understand your guilt feelings? Will you understand his?

➤ Will you be jealous of his desire to spend time with old friends or friends from work? Will he resent your reunions with your friends?

➤ How will you react if his job takes priority over other plans? How will he react if your job takes priority?

➤ In what areas do you need to feel superior to him or to other individuals in his life? When do you need him to be superior to you or to others?

➤ Can you share family obligations, whether to your family or his, or to the children you'll have, and do this without resentment?

➤ Do you have a desire to travel, to explore, or to seek art and culture? Does he have these feelings?

➤ What about religion and spirituality? Does he feel as strongly as you do?

Meeting Needs

Every person has four primary kinds of needs: physical, intellectual, emotional, and goal-oriented. Let's see how mutual fulfillment of these needs can create bonding with your man.

1. *Physical needs.* Fulfill the man's physical needs by providing comforts. Make sure he has proper rest and healthful activities, and expect him to do the same for you. Provide stimulation for all five senses. Most definitely, in time, include sex.

2. *Intellectual needs.* Each of us needs to be with a similarly intelligent mate; otherwise, we'll feel alone. Match his intellectual expectations and expect the same from him. If you don't know as much about something as he does, ask him to teach you. Do the same for him.

3. *Emotional needs.* Fulfill the man's emotional needs, stimulated with praise and criticism. He'll become frustrated or bored if you fail to stimulate these emotions—and you're likely to lose him if he's bored. He should also be fulfilling your emotional needs, and he may very well lose you if he fails to do this.

4. *Goal-oriented needs.* Help your fellow achieve those goals that he believes he must reach at any cost. If you hinder rather than help him, he will pass you by for marriage. He should be helping you achieve your goals, too.

Using Desires to Create and Fulfill Needs

Your likelihood of success in fulfilling his needs and desires is greater if these needs and desires are unique and you are uniquely qualified to fulfill them. To uncover and discover his needs and desires, probe into his motivations for independence, especially as a youngster, and his long-term goals. Remember, you can elicit this information most effectively if you ask first about the past, then the future, and finally the present.

> ➤ If you're an expert shopper, show your man that his wardrobe needs updating. He'll ask you to select his new clothes.
> ➤ If you're a musician, show your man that the play he's writing should be a musical. He'll ask you to write the musical score.
> ➤ If you're a travel photographer, show your man that his architectural designs need a more worldly view. He'll seek to join you on your trips.
> ➤ If you're artistic, show your man that his stationery and business cards are obsolete. He'll ask you to design his stationery and business cards.

A woman who truly wants a man will encourage him to rely on her to enhance his life. She will become indispensable for his comfort and sense of well-being. The man will learn to do this in return, especially if he realizes how much he enjoys you. Teach him what he can count on from you. Of course, if the dependency is too great in either direction, you may be unsuitable as mates.

Be Indispensable

One of the most important techniques for leading a man into marriage is to become indispensable to him. Being indispensable does not mean being subservient. Avoid menial tasks unless they're essential or you genuinely enjoy doing them. While you're making yourself indispensable to him, ask yourself how he's making himself indispensable to you.

Here are some ways in which you can become indispensable to your fellow:

➤ Edit his reports, and improve upon his presentations.

➤ Cook his favorite meal at least once a week.

➤ Select clothing for him that makes him look great.

➤ Sort his bills, balance his checkbook, and prepare his financial plan.

➤ Help him to keep current with political ideas, or to articulate these views to others.

➤ Get to know his family, friends, and business contacts so that you can be together on social and business occasions.

➤ Be willing to help in emergencies with his family or job.

➤ Participate in his hobbies—be a fourth for bridge or tennis even if you don't particularly like those games.

➤ Make constructive criticisms, but only in private.

➤ Tell the world how wonderful he is—be his public relations person.

There are deep differences among individuals, especially when it comes to marriage and family. An act that one person would consider indispensable, someone else would consider annoying or worse. Before you attempt to make yourself indispensable to a particular man, discover his particular needs. Do this when you interview him. Remember, desires are different from needs, so focus first upon his needs when you can. Then look to his desires and yours.

His Need to Be Needed

If your man is like most men, he wants to be needed. In fact, he *needs* to be needed. He may even stay with a woman he doesn't truly want because she needs him. If a woman doesn't show need for a man, he may avoid a relationship with her, even if he wants her. If you want him, show your need for him.

What is this "need to be needed"? Is it chivalry, male chauvinism, or some entirely different phenomenon? In fact, it's the reverse of chivalry or even male chauvinism. This need relates directly to male insecurities and the rejection that boys suffered during adolescence at the hands of girls.

Men fear rejection by women. They want to minimize their risk of rejection. A man seeks a woman who needs him because this woman is less likely to reject him. If you ask a typical man, "Why do you want to marry a woman who needs you?" he will respond, "If she doesn't need me, she might leave me."

To see his reaction, imagine that a famous celebrity asked you for marriage. Initially, you'd be ecstatic, but then you'd start to wonder whether other women would be chasing him successfully. You'd soon come to feel that your marriage is in jeopardy. You'd feel safe in your marriage only if he was dependent on you for something very important. A man needs this same sense of security before he marries.

An insecure man may offer a woman furs, jewelry, or other worldly goods in his attempt to obtain her loyalty. The more insecure the man, the more he feels the need to buy the woman's attention and affection with possessions. His unconscious strategy is to induce the woman to need him and become dependent on him. Yet he cannot buy genuine love.

Don't be afraid of saying to a man, "I need you to do this for me!" If it's not an overwhelming burden to him, he will respond to your request—but don't exploit him. He will want you to be appreciative of his efforts and benefit from his talents. So balance what he does for you by doing "your thing" for him.

The man needs some assurance that he is irreplaceable in your life, so that it is safe for him to love you. He knows you will not readily pull away from commitment if you need him. The man also enjoys the ego recognition that comes from feeling so needed. "Honey, I can't imagine life without you" goes a long way. But don't become a burden. That's *not* what he wants.

Successful Independence

You achieve interdependence when two things happen: You begin to depend on him for the things he does best and will do willingly, and he begins to depend on you for things you do best and will do willingly. Sit down with your future mate and discuss how you enrich each other's lives. Think about the areas in which you and he complement each other. Does he fulfill enough of your needs to make you a happier person? Do you fulfill his needs to the point that he is delighted with you? Balance the added effort it takes to have a mate with the added comforts that having a mate provides. Your life and his should be happier as a result of your togetherness.

Marriage is a lot like getting into a lifeboat with your mate. You should be sure that both of you will row in the same direction, and that neither of you will drop anchor or row in the opposite direction. The more you help him in achieving his goals, and the more he helps you in achieving yours, the greater the probability is that you will have a successful marriage.

MARRIAGE ATTITUDES

A man expects certain attitudes from his wife. You need to display these attitudes to him if you are serious about marriage. Then, as a woman, you are expecting certain attitudes from your future husband. Consider now if his marriage attitudes are compatible with yours.

Work

Most men have to work for a living. In their work, they deal with an outside world that often is exhausting and frustrating. A man expects to work to support himself and may expect the same from his wife. Show your willingness to help him or to work for a living. Don't be a weight around his neck or a prima donna who won't pitch in.

Demonstrate to the man that you are an asset, not a liability, that you also have a work ethic, and that you will help in your mutual survival.

Parents

Our parents cared for us when we were youngsters, and the time may come when we may have to care for them when they reach old age. This is the cycle of life, whether we like it or not. The man may have responsibilities to either or both of his parents and may worry that you will resent the time and expense he has to spend on his folks.

It's the duty of one spouse to help the other provide care for elderly parents. It may not be pleasant to sit with your man through the aging and death of his parents, but it's part of your marital duties. Indicate by your own behavior and attitudes toward your own elderly relatives that you will willingly take on this responsibility if it becomes necessary. Expect him to do the same for you.

His Children

The man you want may have children. You have several emotional hurdles to overcome with his children, but his children can become a great source of joy for you, and love you as a second mom.

The female, by nature, usually has strong love instincts for her child, whether or not she really cares for the child's father. The male, on the other hand, initially loves the child to the same degree that he loves the child's mother.

Don't be too surprised if your man doesn't have strong paternal instincts. Some men do, others don't. This doesn't mean you can be indifferent to his children, however. Treat his children in a very loving manner, as if you were their mother. Remember, if you marry the man, you are expected to be a loving parent to his children and a loving grandparent to his grandchildren.

One of the greatest errors a woman can make is to show hostility to a man's children from a previous marriage. The children are the innocent victims of a love relationship that went sour. Do not criticize their mother in their presence. Any unkind remarks or attitudes toward the natural mother will build their resentment toward you.

Children of broken homes wish that their natural parents would get together again. As kind and as thoughtful as you are to his children, they would still displace you if it meant that their mom and dad had a chance at reconciliation. They may even say so loudly. Don't be offended! Bide your time, for when you marry and the children see that you do not plan to overrun their father or push them out of his life, they will become supportive and respectful of you.

Children require tender love and care as well as expense, patience, and extraordinary energy and time. When you're dealing with his or your children from a previous marriage, the man needs to know that you are a good parent. He'll indicate what he expects a good mother to do and to be. Don't act indifferent, mean, or lacking in joy when you deal with his children or yours; you'll be passed by for marriage if children are important to him, especially if he's looking to start a family. Furthermore, a man will assume that if you are mean to a child, you will also be mean to him.

Pets

Many people identify with pets. If you're cruel to your pet or to his, a man may fear that you're capable of the same cruelty toward him. Turn this concept to your advantage by fussing over any pet, especially his. Even if the man scowls when you fuss with his pet, he will appreciate your considerate behavior and respond as if the kindness were directed at him.

FEATHERING THE FUTURE NEST

You want your future mate to invest time, energy, and emotions in your future. Create fond memories and build your personal history together. Encourage projects that will carry over to a mutual "nest," such as:

> ➤ Building a bookcase.
> ➤ Finding a home or homesite together.
> ➤ Buying electronic equipment together.
> ➤ Refurbishing furniture together.
> ➤ Creating a music library of your favorite songs.
> ➤ Adopting a pet you select together.

Suppose you have a dog and you know he likes dogs. Ask him to wash Rover for you. The first time you do this, he's doing you a favor. The second time, he's doing Rover a favor. The third time, it's "his dog." Let him invest those emotions.

Share the responsibilities of daily life. The more time and energy he invests in you, the more likely he is to continue. If you can balance a checkbook better than he can, do his. If he is a better shopper than you are, let him do the shopping. The more familiar he is with the lifestyle and surroundings he'll have when the two of you marry, the easier the transition will be.

chapter 12

Your Engagement and Wedding

MAKING YOUR SALES PITCH

You know how terrific you are, and how ecstatic a man should be to have you forever. I've asked you to wait in making your "sales pitch" to the man of your choice until you're sure that he's worthy of you; after all, we didn't want you to make that effort for men who don't meet your needs. Now, however, is the time for your sales pitch. Indeed, a man expects this pitch and may think the woman lacks interest in him if he doesn't hear one.

Show your fellow your superiorities over other women. He is likely to diminish your claims, so build up your assertions to compensate. This way you should come out even in his judgment of you.

Some sales managers tell their salespeople, "Throw enough mud against the wall and some of it will stick." Many politicians use the same technique. Enhance yourself and your desirability by throwing enough positive ideas about yourself at him that many will stick.

You can convince the man of your choice to marry you if you make the right sales pitch at the right time. Both timing and substance are crucial. Tell him the many reasons why he should marry you. Let him know that your goals are compatible with his and that you can foresee a happy future together.

Establishing Your Uniqueness

Just as it's important for you to recognize your man's uniqueness, it's important for him to recognize yours. You'll likely have one or more of the following superior features, as well as others:

Good lover	Lively
Optimist	Cultured
Beautiful eyes	A good voice
Good listener	Funster
Neat housekeeper	Musical ability
Good sense of humor	Good in sports
Interesting conversationalist	Superior intelligence
Good cook	Good mother
Kind	Ambitious
Successful in your career	Professional recognition
Firm breasts	Shapely legs
Environmentally responsible	Talent
Good dancer	Frugal
Good genes	Wise
Loyal	Good planner
Family-oriented	Responsible
Well read	Truthful

Ascertain your superior qualities and determine which of them will appeal to the man. Then accentuate these attributes of yours, one at time, until he repeats each attribute back to you as his idea. This is one of the most important steps in selling yourself to him. When you interviewed him for the job of husband, you determined which qualities he was seeking. Now let him know that you have the special qualities he desires.

Getting Him to Think About the Future

Some men take life or work so seriously that they don't devote adequate attention to their women. They don't think about marriage. However, these men can be led toward marriage if you can change their focus.

If your fellow works too hard or takes life more seriously than he should, take him to a cemetery to sober him into reality. This is "shock therapy," designed to let him realize he's not enjoying life to the fullest. Your best bet is to visit the grave of one of his departed relatives. If that isn't feasible, visit a historic graveyard or national cemetery, where visitors are common. You want him to realize that he will not live forever and that he should be thinking about his personal future, including marriage to you. As he reads headstones, he will reflect on his own mortality.

If you can't take your man to a cemetery, use other techniques to remind him of his fleeting existence on earth. Ask him what he'd like his tombstone to say. Ask if he would prefer cremation. Subtly remind him that his next heartbeat may be his last. Start with a comment such as "Isn't it amazing that we go about our lives so casually?" Ask him how much fun he has really experienced so far, and ask him what he'd like to do with the rest of his life.

RAISING THE TOPIC OF MARRIAGE

You want the idea of marriage to occur to your man and for him to bring it up. If he doesn't, use others to bring it up. Don't leave anything to chance. The next best option is for the idea of marriage to be brought up by others. Let the world suggest marriage.

When marriage talk is timely, but he hasn't mentioned marriage plans, go to places where the world will treat the two of you as married. Go browsing or shopping for big-ticket items that he'll enjoy seeing and that are usually bought by married couples. Here are some examples:

➤ Homes
➤ Motor homes
➤ Condominiums
➤ Boats
➤ Cars
➤ Large-screen television sets
➤ Refrigerators
➤ Stoves
➤ Pool tables
➤ Expensive artwork

The salesperson, trying to sell goods, will paint a very rosy picture of you and your husband living at Heavenly Ranch Estates, perhaps pointing out how much your children will enjoy the new television or pool table. Don't bother to correct the salesperson. Instead, wink or look amused at your man. Later you can refer to the fact you two are starting to "look married" and belong together.

Try to become involved with his family occasions. Your goal is to favorably impress his parents and other family members. Meet his aunts and uncles, nieces and nephews. Someone in his family is likely to say, "I wonder what your children would look like?" His family will start him thinking about sharing his life with you.

Describe an optimistic future for him with you in it. Make such statements as, "If you and I combined our efforts and talents, there isn't anything we couldn't accomplish." Talk about the safari you are planning together next year, or the vacation home you both could own in three years. If he wants a beautiful home, pick up a magazine with pictures of desirable houses to fire his imagination. Do the same for other interests he has.

Behave as if you already are married. Let him depend on you as he would depend on a wife, and act as his partner in fighting off the cruel world. Determine his image of the perfect mate and take on the part! If he is in business and must entertain, learn to be a good hostess and help him. Fuss at his dress, tell him his hair needs to be trimmed, comment on his manners, and carry on as you would with a husband. Then expect the same from him.

THE PROPOSAL

Chances are that every married woman you know, especially your mother, told you a tale about how her husband got down on bended knee and romantically asked for her hand in marriage. The truth is likely quite different and more interesting. Chances are that she used her wiles to get her man and that she orchestrated the proposal.

Marriage is not caused by spontaneous combustion. A couple usually reach a point where they act and live as though they are married. Something else must occur for them to actually *decide* to marry. Usually, after being together for six months to a year, it's time to move into marriage. If your partner is spending all his free time with you, the relationship is sexually exclusive, you are openly communicative, and you are living as if you were married, then it's time for a proposal.

If the proposal is left to you, here's how to handle it. Tell your partner, "Honey, I just enjoy life so much when we're together that if you don't propose to me within the next few months, I'll propose to you." The best time of year to get a commitment from a man is late in the year because holidays center on family life. The wedding may take place in the summer, but the commitment is made in November or December. When your man asks you what you want for Christmas, be sure to say "you." Don't say "a ring." This may sound materialistic to a man who is about to give himself to you.

A man brings up marriage indirectly without asking for your commitment, such as saying, "When you and I tire of dating others, it's time to settle down." He may be testing you, expecting you to say, "Why wait? I love you now."

Why does a man do this? He fears rejection, and fears to ask for marriage directly because of the answer he'll receive. Look at your past relationships. Did you miss a marriage opportunity?

Avoid blatant ultimatums, but you don't need to be subtle, either. One woman told her live-in partner, "The next trip we take together will be our honeymoon," and it was. I told my husband in October that he could choose the wedding date as long as it was within that calendar year. We married December 30.

YOUR ENGAGEMENT

Relationships grow and develop into marriage, passing through a number of stages, including the engagement. Your engagement is the transition period between single life and marriage. The engagement begins with the decision to marry, the announcement, perhaps a ring, and includes celebrations, wedding plans, and serious discussions about your future life together.

It takes effort to be engaged, just as it took effort to become engaged. This transition to marriage is often difficult, and many engagements are broken because the woman took the man for granted during the engagement period.

The Ring

You don't need an engagement ring to be engaged, but they are commonplace. Be cautious when selecting a ring. Many women want large diamonds to show off to their friends. Your man, in contrast, might consider a diamond engagement ring a display of greed. Many engagements have ended here. If he does buy you a diamond, put his mind at ease by telling him that the ring is his, and he can have it back at any time. Or show your man that you are considerate of his finances by suggesting cubic zirconium rather than a diamond. Diamonds can come later. Tell him that you will wear the ring proudly, regardless of its price.

If he does bring you a large diamond, he may do so to show off his status and success, or to intimidate other men and make you less approachable. Don't let the ring inflate your ego. Remember, another woman could wear the diamond. The ring neither enhances nor detracts from your true uniqueness.

If your fellow selects the ring, don't have the stone appraised. Don't brag to your friends about how much the ring is worth. Don't let your female friends fuss over the large stone or its worth. The man would be offended by these actions, and the engagement would soon end. Your fellow views himself as the gem he is awarding you. If you place too much emphasis on the ring, he will feel you are diminishing *his* importance.

Maintaining the Engagement

An engagement is an occasion for celebration, but it's also your opportunity to become accustomed to each other. Don't let festivities obscure the reality of daily living. Your man, not your friends, should be first in your life. Don't let your friends overshadow his importance. If he isn't first in your life, don't marry him.

The engagement period should be long enough to prepare for the wedding, but short enough to keep the joy and enthusiasm of your commitment high, typically between three and twelve months. You might have to wait longer if there are constraints such as family and finances, but you'll risk having the engagement itself being a burden. A long engagement period is difficult—you'll have the obligations of marriage without its rewards.

Your fiancé may be shy and may balk at the social frills involved in a wedding. To test your love for him, he may suggest that you elope. If he does make that suggestion, tell him you will! If you truly love him, your focus should be on your marriage, not on your wedding. You might mention that your deposit on the hall may be lost and that friends and family will be disappointed, but do not refuse to elope. Don't marry someone with whom you wouldn't elope.

Sex and Exclusivity

If your relationship has been moving in the right direction, you've been having sexual relations for some time before becoming engaged. Even among those few who oppose sex before marriage, sex during engagement is widely accepted. Sexual relations are essential at this stage unless you're not contemplating sex after marriage, either. You need to determine if you and he can adjust to each other's needs in sex and in other facets of life.

Begin living together while you are engaged if you're not already doing so. Before you're married, you should be sure that you and your man have compatible lifestyles. Try to spend as much time together as possible. If your relationship isn't already sexually exclusive, it should become so once you are engaged.

The Dastardly Act

The man may be angry with himself for falling in love. He may be absolutely enthralled with you, but he may be thinking wistfully of the millions of women he has not yet encountered and must now permanently forgo. In fact, he may be so angry that he may do something mean to you on the brink of marriage. He may, perhaps subconsciously, want to test you to be sure that you really love him. You can ride out the storm if you are prepared for such a "dastardly act." He soon will revert to his sweet, lovable self. Women who don't understand men may misread the dastardly act and end the relationship. He reverts from his good behavior toward you and shows himself at his worst to make sure that you want him even then.

The most extreme dastardly act I have ever seen in the course of developing a marriage relationship was that of a fellow who showed up at his wedding with a date—who was not his bride! The bride introduced the woman to the wedding guests as her fiancé's *last* date, and she was. Even my own husband committed a dastardly act. He refused to wear a tie to our wedding. Whether the act is cruel or just symbolic, realize that it is simply the man's last gesture of resistance before marriage. Don't let yourself react negatively. You're on the right track!

Final Checklist Before Marriage

This is a checklist of crucial information that prospective mates should know about each other before making a marriage commitment. These are twenty-one things you *must* know about the person you marry. Surprisingly, many people who marry don't even know this much about each other, and must face the consequences later.

1. Age
2. Financial obligations, including those to support or care for others, such as former spouses, children, or parents
3. Marital status
4. Children (natural and adopted)
5. Religious beliefs
6. Sexual frequency
7. Financial assets and income
8. Attitude toward each other's ethnic background and cultures
9. Values placed upon family loyalty
10. "Skeletons in the closet" that may later cause public embarrassment
11. Legal situations, such as trials, convictions, and judgments
12. Sexual orientation
13. Education
14. Superstitions

15. Philosophy of life
16. Expectations concerning sexual exclusivity
17. The status of prior serious relationships
18. Spending patterns
19. Health problems
20. Vices
21. Sense of right and wrong

Each prospective spouse has the right to know the true situation of the other person, to determine the probability of a successful marriage and the possible areas of major conflicts. But portions of this information are not always readily ascertainable.

Don't use this checklist at the outset of your dating relationship with him. You should have secured all of these answers before you commit to each other. This is your last clear chance before marriage to get the information you lack. You can't know how to proceed unless you know all the facts.

THE MARRIAGE CONTRACT

For most of us, marriage is the most important legal relationship we will ever enter into, even more important than buying a house or forming a business of our own. You may well find it to your advantage to protect yourself and your future husband through a marriage contract. These contracts are most important when the parties have major disparities in wealth, life expectancy, children from a prior marriage, or other factors.

A marriage contract is an agreement between the future husband and the future wife that identifies their rights, responsibilities, and property ownership; this contract should also settle all questions of financial responsibility between the spouses. Before you get married, a lawyer should help you draw up a marriage contract. Your man will need a lawyer, too.

Welcome the opportunity to have a marriage contract, as it gets both parties to discuss their expectations in a forthright manner. Use this book's checklist of twenty-one items as a starting point.

LIMITING FAMILY INTERFERENCE

You may be facing family interference when you are planning to marry. If so, develop a response to these family members.

If your parents condemn your future husband because of their personal prejudices, don't let them dissuade you. Don't drop him just because they said so. Ask for all the specifics about the objections, writing these objections down if they're long. Don't respond quite yet. Instead, ask if there are more objections. Once all objections are aired, respond to each one. Your mother or another family member could be discouraging you because she is lonely or you've been filling some of her needs. Keep conditioning her to your man. Even if you aren't initially successful, in time she will probably accept him as your husband and treat him as a son.

Your children may object to your marriage, especially if their father is alive and not remarried. His children, too, may oppose your marriage, especially if their mother is alive and not remarried. Don't let them interfere with your marriage plans. Tell them that while you're sorry to hear that they feel this way, you hope that they will come to see that you truly want and need this relationship for your own happiness, and that you hope your happiness is important to them. Children from his previous marriage may be your greatest source of Mother's Day greetings once they learn you are not an ogre who will devour their father.

YOUR WEDDING

Your wedding plans should solidify your relationship and enable you to start your marriage on a strong foundation. All too often, however, an impending wedding weakens rather than strengthens the relationship. In fact, planning your wedding is the last opportunity before marriage to frighten the man into remaining a bachelor.

A woman may mishandle her wedding if she does not keep the interests of her man clearly in mind. Women who make these mistakes are most commonly those who have never been married before. A woman may have fantasized about her wedding from the time she was a young girl. She pictures every detail of the ceremony, from her wedding dress to her bridal bouquet. She knows whom she wants to invite, how she wants the invitations to read, and which guests she wants to sit together. She views the wedding day as *her* day, with little if any thought for the groom and his desires. This attitude will strike the man as immature and selfish. Remember, a wedding is *his* day, too.

The bride's family traditionally made wedding plans and bore the cost of the wedding. Today, however, many women and men have their own idea about the wedding. It's well advised to consider these ideas in making wedding plans. Be sure to consult with the man about major aspects of the wedding ceremony.

Long ago, some women believed that their future husband should not see them in their wedding dress, or should not see them on their wedding day before the ceremony. These traditions are destructive, because it makes the man feel left out of the ceremony and destroys some of the necessary closeness between the man and woman.

A big wedding poses an especially great danger to the relationship. Often, the bride devotes so much time and energy to the wedding plans that she neglects her intended husband. Yet it is at this time that the man most needs her attention and reassurances of her love.

Your wedding is the beginning of your married life, not just the end of your single life. Make it enjoyable for your husband, too. The woman should remember that the wedding day is not her day. It's *their* day!

Now that you've come to the end of the book, you'll be better prepared to accomplish what you've set forth, to meet and marry the man of your choice. Marriage, like anything else that has value in life, takes effort, patience, and nurturing. Keep on trying and testing as you gain experience with men.

Let me know your thoughts and comments and your experiences in using the book. I can't respond to every letter, but I will try.

From time to time I run workshops on getting married and on staying married. Let me know if you are interested in attending.

You now have the knowledge to attract a man you truly want. Turn your dreams to action. Get out there and get the man of your choice!

And, of course, do send me a wedding announcement!

Margaret Kent
www.RomanceRoad.com
multijur@aol.com